IN MY FATHER'S SHOES

Healing the Father Wound

In My Father's Shoes

Healing the Father Wound

By Malik Carey, CEO
with Jack Redmond

ENDORSEMENTS

Malik Carey's story proves that people can change. Life transformation is possible and real. As his pastor for over a decade, I've had the tremendous honor in watching Malik change to become a new man—a man of God. Granted, it took a lot of hard work and determination on Malik's part; all fueled by God's grace and patience. As you read about Malik's journey you will enjoy, as I have, a front row seat in witnessing how a student becomes a teacher, and a teacher becomes a leader in training other men the essential life skill of manhood. In My Father's Shoes *is a must read for men and women who long to fulfill their God-given potential!*

David D. Ireland, Ph.D.

Lead Pastor & Author, *One in Christ; The Kneeling Warrior*

www.DavidIreland.org

Many people go through trying times in life, but few share their stories with others to help them overcome their own personal struggles. Malik Carey candidly opens up his life to show that in spite of all odds stacked against you, you can still come out on top. He discovered who he was through God's eyes and not the stereo type that others put on young men without the guidance of a natural father. Discover how God can take what looks like an impossibility and make it possible through Malik's story of tragedy to triumph. You will discover that God truly makes all things work together for your good.

Apostles Tony & Cynthia Brazelton

Victory Christian Ministries International, www.vcmi.org

After spending only a few moments in the presence of Malik Carey, one cannot help but sense his great passion for God and for life. Yet this infec-

tious exuberance does not come from a life journey of ease and simplicity, but from the crucible of complexity and challenges that this brother has uniquely overcome.

From tragedy to triumph, from loss to liberation, from pain to prosperity, Malik's story can inspire a generation of people, particularly men, who sincerely desire to overcome their past and walk in the power of their potential. God has empowered Malik to become an insightful and influential servant and leader, with the unique ability to articulate the struggles that many brothers have suffered. Yet with spiritual depth and practical insight, he guides men into a place of healing and wholeness drawing from the strength of his own testimony. Throughout these pages, Malik opens his HEART in order to give the rest of us HOPE.

Dr. Joseph Bryant
National Sports Director
Co-Director of Diversity in Technology & Regional Field Director for
Rev. Jesse Jackson & The Rainbow PUSH Coalition

The painful reality is that many of our young men and grown men are hurting. They are hurting because their fathers were absent, ineffective or both! The statistics are staggering. Even the men who make it through often struggle in their relationships, careers and then as fathers themselves. Instead of just complaining about current realities, Malik offers both hope and practical solutions to help men leave a painful past and move forward into a more prosperous future. As Malik's big brother, I have watched Malik fall, get up and do it better. He demonstrates that even when it's hard, a better future is possible. He has lived this truth and so can you!

Nino Villanova
Georgia Music Association
President MCA Music

I remember when my oldest son and I were having a conversation in our family jacuzzi. All of a sudden, he jumps up and defiantly screams out, "I don't want to be like you!" I responded by saying, "Son, you are just like me before I surrendered my life to the LORD Jesus. You only know who I am now, a life surrendered to being God's Child." On his 30th birthday, he was baptized, surrendering his life to CHRIST; the same age and time of God's calling as was in my life. Now, he is just like me! This book is a must-read liberating experience for both fathers and sons!

Lee Rouson
2 Time Super Bowl Champion, New York Football Giants

Malik does an awesome job at speaking to the all too familiar story of fatherlessness through the lens of his childhood. In a society where 43% of children are born out of wedlock, this book unveils the pathway to both pain and success. Transparency is the solution to healing. A MUST READ!

Kenneth Braswell
Executive Director of Father's Incorporated

As the founder of Legacy Minded Men, I constantly work with men whose fathers were either absent or ineffective. This leaves many adult men ill-equipped to navigate and succeed in their relationships, marriage, family and careers. Malik's transparency, wisdom and practical steps given are needed for men to not only understand how they got to where they are, but even more importantly how to get to a better place.

Joe Pellegrino
President of Legacy Minded Men
Author of *Transformation, That's My Dad* and *Father's Say*

Malik has given us a very transparent blueprint concerning his personal pains and struggles. His story will help men be honest with themselves and will touch the depths of their heart. It will put men on the path to live the life that God created them to live.

Calvin A Duncan
Senior Pastor, Faith & Family Church

Malik is a very special young man. I have had the joy of mentoring him as he has started and built up the Family Healing Center. His life demonstrates the painful reality of growing up without a father and the devastating consequences it can have. Through many ups and downs, Malik has learned to live a lifestyle of growth that is driven by faith. His life is an example of how God can transform a man. His hard work of returning to school as an adult, then becoming CEO of his own business, shows that life has many opportunities if we will take them. Malik did grow up in his father's shoes repeating many harmful and self-destructive behaviors, but also demonstrates that we have the power to put on our own shoes and walk a better and healthier path.

Bill Powell, MSW

Groundbreaking! Author Malik Carey takes us where some of us may not want to go in his insightful book, In My Father's Shoes: Healing The Father Wound. *In an effort to help readers face the quandary of dealing with their own fathers' mortality, Malik opens his own heart – risking further emotional injury to himself – to help us deal with the pain that each of us will someday have to face. He reminds us that our Heavenly Father sees, understands, and restores.*

Dr. Kenneth T. Whalum, Jr.
The New Olivet Worship Center

My passion to help men has driven me to partner with many organizations, and also to start my own non-profit. Maturing teens and grown men need guidance, but even more importantly inspiration, to do and live better. In My Father's Shoes delivers on both because Malik Carey has lived both. Readers will be encouraged to look at life differently and then live differently. This will impact their own lives, their children's lives and impact society as a whole.

John Blanton
Coach, Founder of Men Make a Difference

I have worked with young men for over 25 years in Special Education and athletics. I have seen many highly intelligent and passionate young men try to navigate life with a lack of a father's guidance. Some have succeeded and too many have failed. I met Malik when we were 12 years old and struggling ourselves without our fathers. Malik demonstrates that how we start is not as important as how we finish. This book is destined to impact many young men leading them to live better lives.

Michael Baldwin, M.A.
Athletic Director, East Orange Public High School

You are born looking like your father, but will die looking like your choices. Malik's story is a demonstration that God has a plan and a purpose for every man and you can live up to your God given potential in spite of any difficult background. Though his life began with many difficult and problem filled chapters, when Malik allowed God to write HIs life story everything changed! In My Father's Shoes is a dispatch to provide hope for tremendous healing!

Rev. Adam Durso
Executive Director, LEAD.NYC
NYC Mayor's Clergy Advisory Council

In My Father's Shoes is a chilling memoir that will expose the unspoken conversations about a man's God-given need for identity, affirmation and purpose. This book's redemptive nature reveals that no experience, no matter how tragic in our lives, will be wasted. All things can work together for our good! Malik's authenticity will cause you to journey with him to re-discover true manhood. It's a "beautiful mess" that will encourage the boy in every man.

Pastor Portia Taylor
Author of *I'm Not That Woman*

IN MY FATHER'S SHOES
Healing the Father Wound

Copyright © 2018 – Malik Carey and Jack Redmond
www.MalikCareyCEO.org | www.JackRedmond.org

COVER CONCEPT: BERNARD WILLIAMS
COVER AND INTERIOR LAYOUT: SWINGHOUSE DESIGN STUDIO
ISBN-13: 978-1727760958 / ISBN-10: 1727760956
PRINTED IN THE UNITED STATES OF AMERICA. MALIK CAREY, CEO

ACKNOWLEDGMENTS

I first want to give honor to my Lord and Savior Jesus Christ, for giving me the strength and courage to tell my story, for saving a broken man and healing the little boy who needed to be healed.

To my son London, you are really growing into a great young man. I am truly proud of you and the man you are becoming. I thank God every day for you.

To my mom Sandra Honore, I want to thank you for always encouraging me to follow my dreams, even when things got tough. You taught me never to give up. Thank you.

To my big brother Nino Villanueva, you taught me how to navigate life at such an early age. We pushed each other to be better and continue to aspire to greater things in life. You taught me never to take no for an answer and most of all, to chase your dreams at all cost and never to give up.

To my brother Daryl Johnson, my right-hand man. Thank you for holding me down in one of the toughest times in my life. I am forever grateful for your love and support through the years. You are everything brotherhood is made of and I love you so much.

To my mother-in-love Patricia Drayton (AKA) P-Diddy, you have supported me from day one when we met. You have been a true confidant and prayer warrior. Most of all you gave me the best wife on the planet! I love you to pieces.

To my best friend Jay Jones, you have been there for me like no other. We have been through thick and thin together. You have shown me what true godly friendship is all about. You are the friend that sticks closer than a brother. Jay, you got saved and came back and snatched me from hell. You prayed for me and loved me until I could love myself. You taught me what a true godly man is like. Jay, you taught me how to forgive and how to serve. Thank you!

To Troy Bowers, you have been a real example of a real godly man. You inspire me daily to make a difference for the body of Christ. Coach Troy, you are a giant for Christ and a true servant.

Chris Broussard, I appreciate you for giving me the opportunity to help you build The K.I.N.G. Movement. You are a true example of a godly man. You taught me how to be a godly husband, father, leader and friend. Chris thank you for everything.

To Pastor Barbara Franklin, you spoke life into me when I was new at Christ Church. You told me I was going to do great things for the Lord. I will never forget that.

To Pastor Anthony Franklin, you taught me how to serve with excellence as your Armor Bearer. You also continue to teach me how to be a godly husband.

To Dr. David Ireland, I thank God for you every day. You and your ministry helped me personally and with my relationship with my dad. Your true humility and transparency about your healing process in your relationship with your father that you shared at a men's conference in 2008 was life changing. Then, when you shared a prophetic word in 2010, you told me that I was going to bring the men in my family to a healing place. Christ Church is where my transformation continues to take place. Pastor Marlinda and you have demonstrated what a godly marriage looks like and my wife and I are so grateful to be under your leadership. Thank you for everything.

To Apostles Tony and Cynthia Brazelton, you have loved on me from day one and I am so blessed to have you as my spiritual parents. Anytime I have called or needed something you have always been there. Your prayers and support go a long way and I love you both so much.

To Pastor Jack Redmond, for coming along side me, as a friend and brother, to help complete this project. You have become a brother from another mother. Losing our fathers at the same time, we both needed to do this and God made a way. I am truly blessed to have you in my life and to serve with you here and abroad as your Armor Bearer and brother. Your passion for evangelism is contagious and I know we are going to change many lives together. I love you bro!

I want to also pass on love to everyone who has supported me through my journey. Special thanks to Bernard Williams from MediaPlate and George Rodriguez of swinghouse design studio for all the work you put in to help me complete my project.

To my Family Healing Center staff, thank you for allowing me to be your CEO and for all the hard work you do for our clients.

To Bill Powell, for being that mentor and wise counsel when I needed it most. I appreciate you giving me the opportunity to open up Family Healing Center and calling me to be the CEO.

To CJ Meenan, you have been my spiritual guide and mentor. You have taught me the true meaning of entrepreneurship, friendship and never to give up on my dreams. Thank you CJ for your commitment to my family and I.

Finally, to my Queen Deidra Carey, who holds it down so I could be everything I need to be, starting with being a husband and father. Deidra you are my source of inspiration. You are so loving, supportive, and caring. I couldn't do any of this without you.

DEDICATION

This book is dedicated to my father, Joseph Lee Randleman.

God chose you to be my father and I am so grateful HE did. You were a true servant of the Lord and it's because of you that I have life. I am blessed to have found you and I thank God that we had our time together to help heal one another. I am the one they say is most like you. I hope this book makes you proud. I love you dad and your spirit always shines upon me.

CONTENTS

FOREWORD

History tells us. Biology tells us. Religion tells us. Statistics tell us. Now, one man – one bruised, broken, completely transparent and utterly inspirational man – is telling us: Fatherhood matters. At a time when America is awash with the devastating effects of fatherlessness, Malik Carey puts a personal face and story on the issue.

For decades, we've read about the results this social plague has on its innocent victims, the children left behind or unattended to by their biological fathers. They're more likely to be poor, more likely to abuse drugs and alcohol, more likely to drop out of school, more likely to be emotionally disturbed, more likely to commit crimes, more likely to be incarcerated. But after years, decades even, of reading and hearing the statistics, we've become numb to them. Hardened by the near normalization of fatherlessness – more than 40% of American children are now born to unwed mothers – we've thrown up our hands and all but yelled a collective, "We give!" With seemingly no answers and no end to this trend in sight, some, perhaps with good intentions, are seeking to diminish the impact of this epidemic. Being raised without a father is not that bad, they say. As long as some adult, regardless of blood relationship or gender, is there, the child will be fine, they say.

But Malik Carey begs to differ. With refreshing candor and honesty, Carey rips the cover off such sentiments. He doesn't deny that one can become materially or financially successful without knowing their father, for he did that. But he shows that career success cannot heal the wounds this situation creates. In what may appear to be a healthy individual because of a high degree of academic, business, or monetary attainment may actually reside a fearful and damaged child in need of fatherly validation.

Carey is not theorizing. He lived it, finding that no amount of achievement, no amount of money, no amount of promiscuous and "macho" behavior, could make whole a man who grew up longing for a relationship with his dad. Try as he did, he could never run from the incessant questions and emotional torment his abandonment brought.

Thankfully, Carey does not leave us wallowing in sadness; for his story is one of redemption. First, he doesn't beat up on his dad or on any man who is not in the life of his children. Understanding that many absent fathers were themselves victims of fatherlessness, he displays uncommon compassion and forgiveness for those in this condition. They need healing too, he writes, having witnessed and realized that the man he grew up wondering about was just as lost as he once had been. Next, Carey offers insight, both spiritual and clinical, into how both father and child can be healed. It is this component that separates *In My Father's Shoes* from your typical memoir. Chock full of advice, insight, and incidents that many will find all too familiar, Carey's book is therapeutic.

I am more than a fan of Carey's story. I am his friend. Having known Malik for more than 10 years, I have personally witnessed his transformation and growth. I have also come to appreciate and admire his incredible openness. Men are notorious for keeping their feelings to themselves, especially their less than flattering ones. Not so with Malik. Through his time as both a patient and a sponsor in a 12-step program, he has learned the power of transparency. No sin, no slight, no embarrassment, is too shameful for him to share. In this, he finds healing. And as you read his book, as you feel his pain, as you identify with his thoughts and experiences, so too will you.

Chris Broussard
FOX Sports TV and Radio Personality
Founder and President, The K.I.N.G. Movement

INTRODUCTION

In My Father's Shoes is the life story of Malik Carey. It is a story of tragedy and triumph, rejection and reconciliation and most importantly, transformation. Like a lot of stories, it's about a road well-traveled with detours, pitfalls, mountain highs and valley lows. There is laughter, tears, too few wins and too many losses. It is a painful story that no one would willingly choose for their life, but a beautiful story in the end. It is a journey, perhaps, similar to the one you are currently on.

WE DON'T CHOOSE OUR PARENTS

This story is about a father who did not choose his son. Chaos, confusion and conflict were the result. As a boy and a young man, Malik often wondered about the man he was always told he was "just like" and frequently questioned how he could be so much like a man he never met.

Somehow, this young man began to find his way. First, he found his way into manhood and much of the world's success. He found his way into the married life, business ownership, and the envy of many. But there was a gaping hole in his life and in his heart that nothing and no one could fill. Maybe it was a gap that was never filled by his father. This hole led to living a double life. Success, women and prestige on one side; drugs, alcohol, divorce and six aborted babies on the other side. Feelings of great success were often drowned out by feelings of failure, stemming from a near death experience, a second time in jail, divorce and the gaping hole that remained.

However, new days brought new possibilities. Despite major odds, new life was given. Through a chance circumstance, father and son were reunited. Malik finally had a chance to know the man he had always been compared to. So, the healing began, with the father he never knew and the new wife with whom God had blessed him. The road was often bumpy but, at least it was moving forward. And with the formation of two new relationships, first with Malik's Heavenly Father and secondly, his earthly father, that gaping hole began to shrink and the gaps began to fill. A young man who was fast becoming a statistic, grew to become a strong man who now lives each day in victory. His story is one of hope and how a better future is available, if we have the courage to take a different road...

SECTION 1

The Early Years

CHAPTER 1

WHO AM I?

*My father gave me the greatest gift anyone could give
another person, he believed in me.*[1]

-JIM VALVANO

Growing up without a father is one of the most painful experiences a
young boy can face. I should know; I personally dealt with this pain in my
own life. Every boy needs and desires a strong male figure to glean from,
to hear "I'm proud of you!" or "You're the greatest!" The great basketball
coach Jim Valvano points to his father believing in him as the greatest
gift he could have received. I never had that; I grew up without my father
believing in me, without him even being around me.

For years I wanted nothing more, only my father. I wanted to know
the man I was supposed to be so much like. The one my mother would
constantly remind me about. Why was she doing that? Was my mother's
own pain and frustration the cause for the constant reminders of an unknown man or was I really that much like him?

The problem is no one knew where this man was. So, questions like "is
he near or is he far?" invaded my mind. Why didn't this dude take care of

me and my sister? Do I have other brothers and sisters, and if so, where are they? These thoughts constantly ran through my mind. I would day-dream about having a father I could throw a football and baseball with, someone I could have a one-on-one conversation with about what it takes to grow up and be a man. Someone who could prepare me for manhood. I wanted these things so bad but instead I was left figuring these things out alone like so many of the other men I hung out with who grew up without their fathers.

BLIND LEADING THE BLIND

It was and is like the blind leading the blind. We were all trying to figure out "manhood", but the real problem was we had no one to teach us. Some of us turned to an uncle or an older friend to help us, but many of the people we turned to didn't have fathers in their lives either. They gave us misguided information, so the quest for manhood continued. Then we *figured it out*; as we got older, we could look to women to validate our manhood. The more women we could have, the manlier we could become. And being macho around each other further proved that we were real men, walking in true manhood. That's what we thought.

But, we were still hurting. To make matters worse, we damaged and scarred our women emotionally and spiritually. Many of them had also grown up without a father in their lives; they were looking to us to guide and direct them, but we couldn't because *no one taught us*, and we didn't know how to treat them. No one taught us about women's value nor their right to be treated with exceptional care. On the contrary, the world told us they were objects for sexual pleasure; we were encouraged to disregard their feelings and emotions.

As men, we are supposed to learn how to treat women, based on how our father's treat our mothers. But, it's hard to learn how to do that or have loving values instilled when no father is present. As a result, I became a womanizer; that's what I was taught by an older friend and an uncle. Years later I would discover my father was the same way. He had many children, by many different women. The days of my mother telling me I was *just like my father* were becoming more and more of a reality.

SO PEOPLE FLOUNDER

Have you ever seen a fish flop on the ground when it is out of water? Over time, a fish flopping on the ground became known as "floundering". It looks funny, but in reality, the fish is frantically trying to breath. It's suffocating as a result of being ripped out of its safe atmosphere with no warning and no ability to fix the situation. Growing up without a father leaves many young men like that fish, never understanding the safety of a good father and the atmosphere it can provide.

Floundering actually means to "struggle or stagger helplessly or clumsily in water or mud" or "struggle mentally; show or feel great confusion" or "be in serious difficulty."[2] Growing up without a father leads to so many young men struggling and staggering through life. They often make many poor decisions in their youth as they struggle mentally and feel great confusion. It's like when you take a test but missed the class where they taught the material on the test, and you never got the information. You guess, hoping it's right, but inside you worry because you really don't know. Growing up without a father teaching you often leads to getting things wrong or failing situations in life because your father was the absent teacher who never gave you the information for the test. Unfortunately, life is not a math or science test, and not knowing the information or not knowing who you are can be devastating. Some drop out of school, but there is no dropping out of life. You still have to live.

IDENTIFYING WITH WHO?

Most people don't know who they are; they know a lot of things, but not who they are. The world tells them many things. People define things as they see fit. Most of us put on a show, but deep in our souls, we have more questions than answers. Many of the strongest, most successful men are broken little boys on the inside. Many men spend their lives trying to find approval from the father that isn't there. It's a painful game we play because there is a gap that nothing else can fill. I believe God has wired us to want to be like our dads so when we don't know what that means, it's like trying to hit a target in the dark.

Many men are looking around for the fathers they have never met. If you are feeling this way, you are not alone. In many circles, you are not the outcast, you are the norm. Even the world will tell you that you are less valuable, or different because of your situation, but you are not. And this is not just about men; my wife never met her father. At 44 years old, as she searched for him, she found an obituary; this is how she learned about her dad. Both men and women ask this question because the one who was supposed to be the strongest, most dependable person was never there. One of the roles of the father is to help children define themselves and reinforce all that is good about them. Without this affirmation, many struggle with who they are. Many wonder if they are really good in a world that points to their failures and magnifies them to the world.

The hard thing about it is that all the success in the world can't fill in the empty spaces and questions of a child that were never answered by their father. It's like life is a puzzle and your dad is holding certain pieces, and for many of us, he is not there to put those pieces where they need to go. So, when we look at life, we really can't see a clear picture because many of the key pieces simply aren't there.

YOU ARE JUST LIKE YOUR FATHER

My mother told me that many times. When I made my mom smile, she would laugh and tell me I was just like my father. When I did something wrong I was, "just like my father". So, I wondered who I got my identity from. I wondered who he really was, who I really was. She told me I looked like him and I wanted to see him, to see if she was right. I wanted to know this man I was supposed to be so much like. There were nights when I would lay awake wondering where he was, what he was doing, and why he chose to leave.

Actually, he never left me, because he was never there. He dated my mom for two years and disappeared sometime after he found out she was pregnant. Even though I had never met him, I still self-identified as *his son*. When my stepfather would discipline me or argue with me, I would yell, "You are not my father!" You see, there is something in boys, a loyalty to our fathers, a desire to be taught by our fathers, to be disciplined by them and yes, to be like them. Feeling this way doesn't make you weak. You are not weak, you are longing to be strong, to be strong like your dad.

DAD, WHY DIDN'T YOU PICK ME FOR YOUR TEAM?

For me, it felt like I was wearing the team jersey, but I wasn't really on the team. I had the uniform and I looked the part, but there was no coach to lead the team. Worst of all, when you are on a team, you are picked to be on the team. I felt like the kid who was on the sideline and never got picked. Why didn't my dad pick me? Why didn't he want me? I didn't question my worth, but many believe if they are not wanted, they are not worth being wanted. These are some of the lies that people think and wrestle with because their fathers were not there to tell them they are valuable, smart, strong and important.

LOOKING GOOD ON THE OUTSIDE

Statistics show that young men who grow up without fathers drop out of school more, are involved with more crime and have less achievements. In today's culture, they often continue the process at an even younger age by fathering children. Another common picture is the man who is strong, educated and doing well on the outside but still hurting on the inside. Many men do well, but in times of crisis or making decisions, they make bad choices and further damage themselves, their family and painfully, the next generation. You may be one of those men who look great on the outside but hide brokenness on the inside. That is my story. I looked great on the outside but didn't know who I was on the inside. I had to learn that my father's absence didn't define me but his strengths did. I also learned that the greatest definition of who I am did not rest on my earthly father, but on my Heavenly Father.

CHAPTER 2

THE ADOLESCENT MAN

Some people grow old, but they never grow up...

-JACK REDMOND

My father died as a 74-year-old adolescent. I loved him dearly, but he literally lived like a teenager in an old man's body. He was a physically grown man and came to be a great man in many ways, but somehow, he never matured. You may be trying to define exactly what an adolescent or what adolescence is. Let's look at an official definition:

Definition of adolescent

1: of, relating to, or being in adolescence

2: emotionally or intellectually immature[3]

So, by definition, an adolescent is immature. Adolescence isn't bad. Seventh graders are supposed to be overly emotional and think the world revolves around them. It's just where they are at in their development. Adolescents are often self-centered, unable to understand that their actions have real consequences and are often driven by impulse without thinking of how their actions will affect others, or even themselves in the long run. Just picture the junior high lunchroom or the Friday night party when someone's parents go out of town. Adolescence at its finest!

Another definition for adolescence: Adolescence begins with the onset of physiologically normal puberty, and ends when an adult identity and behavior are accepted. This period of development corresponds roughly to the period between the ages of 10 and 19 years, which is consistent with the World Health Organization's definition of adolescence.[4] In short adolescence is when hormones are in full force without the maturity or experience to properly handle them at times. That's why parenting is so needed and often the toughest during this period.

WHEN A SHORT STAGE ISN'T SO SHORT

So, we can see that adolescence is a normal part of development. It is actually healthy stage that is one of the funnest parts of life. Little responsibility, lots of energy and real life is still a distant thought for many in this stage. How many of us wouldn't trade our adult responsibilities for those of a 14-year-old for a week? Oh yeah – it's called vacation. The key thing though, is that it is a stage, a transitional time between childhood and adulthood. Supposedly, it "ends when adult identity and behaviour are accepted" by an individual as they transition into adulthood. Legally, people are adults at 18 in America, meaning they can vote and be held accountable for their actions. While legal and physical definitions can be clear, the mental, emotional and behavioral standards can be very blurry for many. Remember adolescence is supposed to be a "stage" of life:

adolescence [ad-l-**es**-*uh* ns]
noun:
1. the transitional period between puberty and adulthood in human development, extending mainly over the teen years and terminating legally when the age of maturity is reached; youth.

2. the process or state of growing to maturity.
3. a period or stage of development, as of a society, preceding maturity.[5]

The adolescent man is someone stuck in their past and often in their pain. They never grow up and they never commit. They make babies and do not take care of them. They don't know how to be a committed husband to their wife or even how to thrive in a committed relationship. They party and drink because they don't know how to handle life or pain without self-medicating through sex, alcohol, drugs or all of the above. These men talk about their past and define themselves by their *Glory Days* and never step into the present or future. They are stuck in adolescence. There is actually a medical term for being stuck; it's called arrested development in the medical and psychological fields:

1. **medicine** - physical development that is not complete
2. **psychology** - psychological development that is not complete[6]

I am currently in my forties. I have peers who've passed through adolescence, into adulthood and are living great lives. I also have peers who are stuck somewhere between junior year of high school and the road trip they took sophomore year in college. This is not limited to my experience but rampant in our society. I wonder how many "mid-life crisis" are just one last chance to be a teenager by someone who never made the emotional transition. I also see many men who can't even have a mid-life crisis because that requires a level of maturity and responsibility, to walk away from, that many have never achieved.

I have sat on planes and talked to grown men who talk about women like a 15-year-old kid trying to get in the pants of an 8th grader. Others have tried to "get deep" about life at 50 years old in a drunken stupor that would make a college freshman jealous.

SO HOW DID WE GET A BUNCH OF BABY HUEY'S?

Baby Huey was a famous cartoon character who was actually a huge baby duck, bigger than most grown men. It was funny because Baby Huey was such a big baby! He was the size of an adult but was still in a diaper and besides his size, he was emotionally and behaviorally a baby. That's why the cartoon was funny.

But these men walking around like Baby Hueys are not funny to their children, their wives, baby mamas, or society as a whole.

How did we get here? We got here, one man at a time, without a father to teach them how to be a man. Let's be real, many men who did have a father around also grew up to be Baby Hueys. On one hand, men, we need to man up. On the other hand, many grown men are struggling and need help to become the men God created them to be.

HOW DO WE HELP OUR MEN MOVE PAST ADOLESCENCE?

Well, easier said than done. It begins with a choice. I had to choose to be grown! I had to look in the mirror and wrestle with every insecurity and start to move forward. Here are a few things I needed to do:

I HAD TO BECOME SICK AND TIRED OF WHAT I HAD BECOME

I had to admit that when I looked in the mirror, I didn't like what I saw. I had to painfully admit that I was a big baby going nowhere. One time, I looked in the mirror and literally saw this beast-like thing looking back. I don't know what that was, maybe how I saw myself, maybe God showing me what I looked like on the inside. In reality, it scared me. I scared me!

Remember, on the outside, I was tall dark and handsome, and could have just about any woman I wanted; but on the inside, I was a mess on a good day and a disaster on a bad day!

I HAD TO REDEFINE WHO I WAS

You can't move forward unless you are willing to let go of the past. I had to learn to see myself differently and to think differently if I was really going to change. I had to reject how the world defined me and how I defined myself. I decided that I would not be defined by my next sexual escapade, new car, or expensive bottles of champagne. It was a change that took time, a true process.

For me, I turned to God and let Him redefine me. I also turned to Him to transform my mind because it had been shaped and molded in so many wrong ways by the world I lived in. It's funny how accurately God's Word identifies our need to think and live differently.

And do not be conformed to this world, but be transformed by the renewing of your mind, so that you may prove what the will of God is, that which is good and acceptable and perfect. -ROMANS 12:2

You see, being stuck in adolescence is never God's will for anyone. It is a stage to be enjoyed but we are to progress out of it. If I did not want to walk in my father's shoes and die a really cool adolescent with gray hair, I would have to stop letting my flesh define me, especially if I wanted to live out God's will for my life. In addition to God, I needed godly men to teach me how to be a man.

I SURROUNDED MYSELF WITH GOOD MEN

The reality is that only a man can teach someone to be a man. No offense to women, but they are not supposed to be able to teach a boy how to be a man. They can teach boys many things and my mother did, but I had no man to guide me into manhood. In fact, I had no real good models to learn from until well into adulthood. My stepdad had some good qualities, but they were drowned out by his bad qualities and my rebellion towards him. It was in my church where I met men, real men, who were faithful to their wives and children and showed me a better way.

DISCOVERING THERE IS A DIFFERENT WAY

I was 34 years old before I met any men that had not cheated on their wives! It happened when I started going to my church. Right now, I know ten male pastors at our church who lead by example in faithfulness to their wives. There are also many men who model commitment and faithfulness. Before joining my church, I literally did not think a man could be faithful to one woman. Today, I am 100% committed to being faithful to my wife. This only made sense to me after God transformed my mind and I was able to be encouraged by other faithful men who became part of my journey.

CHAPTER 3

A View From a Counselor's World

This chapter captures an interview with one of my mentors, Bill Powell, MSW. Bill brings a wealth of expertise and real-world experience from almost four decades of serving predominately African-American families in northern New Jersey. I bring out these details to recognize the unique experience of black families and also to come against the cultural stigma of counseling that exists within my culture.

Yes, challenges that African-Americans deal with are present in all cultures, but let us not be naïve to the realities of the historical social forces of slavery, lack of civil rights and an overdependence and push into the social welfare systems that have damaged the strength of the African-American family in America. Yes, personal choice and responsibility are needed and many people have damaged themselves, their families and society by poor decisions, but the reality of our history has set up a climate that has been damaging towards the African-American family structure.

Bill has combated and helped countless individuals to overcome personal challenges and to fill in the gaps of poor or absentee fathers. We hope you are also able to gleen from his wisdom and also to open up to the possibility of counseling to help you heal and grow to overcome past hurts and move into a better future. This interview has been captured in a question/answer format. Enjoy....

Q *What are the greatest effects you have seen clinically from fatherlessness and/or bad fathering?*

A I have seen many detrimental effects resulting from either absentee or bad fathering. These include poor relational skills that create anger and hostility in their own relationships. These often continued into self-destructive behaviors and actions that hurt their girlfriends, wives and/or children. These men often struggle with resentment and often with depression as they find themselves ill-equipped to navigate the stresses of life and especially in the closeness of relationships. These powerful negative emotions combined with poor interpersonal skills often lead to very tumultuous and unstable relationships both inside and outside the family. These men still function on different levels, and many are successful in multiple areas of life, but it is painful to watch men struggle because they have been hurt and lack the understanding or skills to build strong, healthy relationships. I have seen many men be very successful in their careers and finances, but it means little when their relationship with their wives and children don't go well.

Q *What are some initial thoughts on boys growing up without a father in the house?*

A Men who have grown up without their father have more difficulty in developing strong, healthy relationships. Boys are wired to want to be like their father and imitate what they do. When this is missing, it's like putting together a complicated piece of furniture or a machine without any directions or knowledge. Rarely would this end up well.

You need both male and female to have stability in relationships with the opposite sex because we learn from our environment. When a boy doesn't see his father care, love, protect and provide for his mother and siblings, the boy is missing these subconscious expectations and norms needed when it comes time to have relationships with females. The values, priorities are simply not there. Even if the concepts exist, the boy has missed seeing how they work in real life. Watching a father work, struggle, make mistakes but keep going, sets the tone for a young man.

It is very detrimental to be raised without the father. I do not think this can be underestimated. Even with the most diligent and excellent mother, a fatherless boy will have gaps and damage that most likely will be repeated and grow without significant purposeful intervention and growth.

Q **What percentage of men would you say have been damaged by bad/absent fathers?**

A Most men I see have not grown up with a father or father relationship, probably in the range of 60-70%. Having an intact family is needed for the stability of any individual as both parents are important and their presence dramatically makes life less problematic. I have worked predominately with black families, but any separation between a child and their parent has an effect on a child. This separation or absence is detrimental to a child's development due to the bond being absent or broken.

Many children suffer from depression when their parents are not together. Both individual and family counseling is needed to help each person and the family, that is together, navigate the challenges of life.

This not only effects men but woman also. A girl that knows how to love her father will find a much easier time loving her husband. Since many single mothers have been deeply wounded, there is a kind of double up of damage that takes place as many mothers have unstable relationships. So, a young girl does not learn how to love her father and then sees her mother's pain and unstable relationships which can be very confusing, resulting in a cycle that often repeats itself without significant intervention and counseling.

Q *Does the gap of fatherlessness diminish or disappear with age?*

A Sometimes, but not by itself. I believe two key things are needed. First is divine intervention. God can do things that no amount of talking or counseling can do. This goes way beyond going to church. I am speaking about God's supernatural healing and also through reading of the Bible and letting God change the way you think and understand the world. The second thing is growth. This is most effective when professional therapy is received along with learning of practical relational skills. It must be both spiritual and natural.

Without both things, the result is continual poor relationships which only magnifies the problems, causing many to turn to drugs and alcohol to cope. Unfortunately, built up frustration coupled with a lack of practical relational skills often leads to domestic violence.

Q *So, what is your advice to people who want to live better and have better relationships?*

A Over the decades, I have settled in on five basic principles to help people overcome the gaps and damage of fatherlessness.

BILL POWELL'S 5 RULES TO LIVE BY:

1 **God helps those who help themselves. Do nothing – get nothing.**

You need to get help, but that's up to you. Too many people are waiting around for someone else to fix society or their life. People have to choose to do something different if they want something different. The reality is that many families are dysfunctional. Those wounds from childhood need to be addressed by psychotherapy and counseling to help a person become healthier and a better human being. To say it another way, this means to be closer to being like Christ.

This is more than behavior modification, this is transformation from the inside out so that we can become who God created us to be. I believe there is a powerful effect when a person allows God to be a part of their healing and learning process.

2 **God works in mysterious ways – His wonders to perform.**

When we invite God to be part of our journey and process, He does things that are beyond comprehension. I have seen God take away pain, anger and bitterness in ways that counseling alone never could. I have seen this over and over again for decades. When we surrender our lives to God, we become clay in His hands and He can reshape and remake us.

3 **You take one step – God will take two.**

I've watched over and over again that you can never outdo God! He is a loving Father that is waiting for His children to be ready for help. He doesn't force Himself on people but is ever-ready to step in to help us heal and grow. He created each of us with a purpose and a plan, and He will do mighty things to get us there. But it begins with each person, they have to want to grow, to heal, to change.

4 **The power of life and death is in the tongue – spoken word.**
This saying comes from Proverbs 18:21 – *"The tongue has the power of life and death."* I have watched people transform or sabotage their lives through the words they speak. This goes for both the words we listen to and those we speak. What you say or listen to can literally speak your future into existence. I see so much damage to people's psyche from what people have spoken over them. What you hear can echo in your head and shape you if you let it. People must learn to speak their futures into existence. This doesn't deny a current reality but simply paves the way for a better reality in the days ahead.

5 **We walk by faith, not by sight.**
Many people never move forward into a better life because they can only see their current pain. We often have to look past our current reality to see a better future. We often must see a different future before we are able to make needed behavioral changes, but once we have the faith for a better future, we will often make the needed changes. Going to church and choosing to follow Christ won't make a difference if you go back to the same stuff. The reality is that we will often have to keep moving forward before we can see significant change in either ourselves or our relationships.

Many of us are trying to overcome generations of damage that has either been inflicted upon us or chosen by us through our own bad choices or those of our ancestors. This requires a season of healing that many people never go through. They keep going, but they are like an injured athlete that can still run and even win at times, but ultimately, they are creating more damage unless they take the time to heal. Even taking time to heal takes faith because we are taught that we have to make things happen.

The bottom line is if we want to live better, we have to live more like Christ. In order to become more like Christ – you have to be in a continual state of healing. Every time we are damaged and make choices that damage us more, we become more broken and less like Christ.

Q *What does healing do for people?*

A As we heal the father wounds, we make ourselves more accessible to ourselves and others. This makes us more Christ-like. Jesus is the role model for our relationships. He was always present when He was with people. So much so that the worst sinners, the outcasts, and the most broken people felt at home in His presence.

When we have been psychologically damaged, we are often distant and disconnected even when we are with the people we care most about. The psychological man is damaged through both nature and nurture. Some of our brokenness is through our genetics of personality, pre-disposition towards drugs or alcohol, ease of anger and ways of thinking. Nature is from the biochemical, neurological, genetic make-up – which an individual has no control over. Even though we have no control over what we are given, we have a great deal of control over how we can manage, grow and heal.

Nurture also can cause great psychological damage and a young boy has no control of – because they are conditioned by the environment and behavior of which they are a part. Most boys will simply repeat what they see, especially when they are hormonally driven and have little or no guidance from a strong man to steer them correctly. Each bad decision damages a boy's purity and psychological health. To become closer to Christ and be a better human being – both nature and nurture must be addressed through psychotherapy and counseling as an intricate part of their being.

Unless you deal with the nature and nurture components, a man will be stuck and not be able to achieve success or the goal that Christ has for us – to be whole, wholesome and successful. Every person is damaged both by nature and nurture. Those who come to Christ often need psychotherapy even more because faith can cause you to cover it up and not address it. Some things can be healed in prayer, but my experience has taught me that there are many natural and behavioral things that need to be addressed deeply in conversation and behavioral change. Psychotherapy doesn't take away the need or power of prayer but adds to it by addressing natural issues. If somebody is malnourished, you can pray all day for them but giving them the proper nutrients will still be needed. No one would expect prayer to take away the daily need for protein, carbohydrates, vitamins, and minerals from food, so people should see the need for natural therapy.

Psychotherapy addresses residual things that need to be cleansed and healed. Even when there is external change, behavior, thinking, etc. still needs work. An individual should always be working to better themselves. Like an automobile needs maintenance, so do we. We also need to continually grow closer to Christ. Conversion is one thing, growth is a process.

COUPLES ARE OFTEN JUST TWO BROKEN PEOPLE COMING TOGETHER

Then you have two people coming together with nature/nurture damage – there can be an explosion because people don't understand themselves. So, you have one person who doesn't understand themselves trying to figure out someone who also doesn't understand themselves; it's like mixing two chemicals together which creates a toxic mixture that can be very damaging and even explosive! It often takes psychotherapy to deal with these issues. Without intervention, painful, toxic relationships result which often lead to more broken individuals and families. Unfortunately, many suffer when help is available.

African-Americans have often been taught to "keep it in-house" and not share problems with others and counselors. This thinking is present in all cultures but particularly strong in African-Americans, but it should not be. In the same way, the African-American population has benefitted from education and treatment from such things as diabetes, cancer screenings, etc., I believe now is the time African-Americans leave this false pride behind and get the help they need. The black family has gone from the norm and role model of families 50-60 years ago to a painful example of what happens when family structure breaks down. It is time for the black family to model strength to a world that needs it and this begins with strong individuals.

Men who grow up with a mother often only internalize female thinking with a belief that women call the shots and are in control. This leads to passivity in men and a lack of leadership within their future household. Instead of the man being a source of stability, strength, and vision, they are often passive and don't give needed leadership and strength that they should. This perpetuates into the next generation and diminishes a man's self-worth and self-esteem often leading to passive-aggressive behaviors.

Q *What is the most important part of healing the Father wound?*

A First, as a man, you must learn how to deal with yourself. You must learn where you are hurt, what triggers anger and what causes you to run away from commitment and stability. You have to learn to walk through pain to get to a better future. You have to be strong enough to admit your weaknesses and ask for help from your friends, wife, counselor, and pastor. The street doesn't teach humility, but God does. If you want street results, do what the street teaches, but if you want God's results, do things His way.

FORGIVENESS IS DIFFERENT FROM WHAT PEOPLE THINK

Forgiveness is often needed to move forward. Forgiveness is messy and complicated but needed to move beyond the past. It doesn't mean accepting people's bad choices and behaviors, but it does mean not letting them hurt us anymore. We must learn to forgive our absent fathers and any type of abuse or neglect received. We must also forgive ourselves for the bad decisions and destructive things we may have done to ourselves or others. But the reality is that true forgiveness is very difficult and complex, and this is why counseling is often needed so that people can walk through the process.

People need therapy and need to talk out issues, wounds, and pain – talk is medicinal. If men don't get the proper medication of therapy, they will often lean on self-medicating through drugs, alcohol, sex, money, gangs, sports or even work in an attempt to numb the pain and produce at least a physical sense of pleasure or success.

Talk is the best medicine a person can have – releases things, make things better – to understand ourselves. Talking things out is therapeutic because it releases inner bitterness and toxins from painful and disappointing experiences. Men who grow up without a father often don't feel good about themselves, and these thoughts and emotions eat away at a man's soul and must be purged from his psyche for him to be emotionally healthy.

So, the bottom line I see that men need is first a personal relationship with Jesus that allows Him to heal and lead us. Secondly, men need professional counseling to actually deal with the issues on psychological and emotional levels. Together, these deal with the spirit, soul, and physicality of a man.

CHAPTER 4

I BECAME A STATISTIC

I often processed my pain by writing poems. It helped me vent about my past, my present and a future that didn't look good. This poem expressed my frustration as I threw questions at God.

What is This All About?

*The inner city got them shook, another brother just snatched
a pocket book.
Gun shots in the air, murders every day and poverty the mentality.
Damn, they don't know there's another way.*

*Our educational system is the worst.
15 minutes up the road, they got all the resources and full courses.*

God, what is this all about?

*Our African people are dying from AIDS and Civil Wars.
Is this all part of the Creator's plan?
Man, my black people seem to have been born with
some type of curse!*

God, what is this all about?
They say God is everywhere present, but where are You in this war
in Iraq?
Young men are coming home in body bags and where are You
in all this poverty?
People are starving all over the world and where are You
in all this government corruption and destruction?

God, what is this all about?

Sometimes, I just want to scream and shout!
And why did You take my brother from me?

Why were we as a people enslaved?
And why did You separate the black man from his family?
And why couldn't we bounce back like the Jews?
Six million of them murdered and they're still tight.
We can't even trust our neighbors at night.

Why are we lost as a people?

Why was I born without my biological father at home?
And why am I not home with my son?
And why does my father have eight children from six
different women?

What's this all about?

Why have I abused sex, drugs and alcohol?

And why is my son here with a mother who has four children
from four different men?

God, where are You? Are You still here?

My family system sucks.
Why is the black family system in such shambles?
Or is this just the way it is?

Why do I have such a hard time in a male-female relationship?
Oh! I know why.
Because my father never taught me how to treat a lady.
He doesn't know how either,
and why is money more important than having a family and
screwing the prettiest woman more important than having
a strong woman by your side.

What is this all about?
God, please tell me what this is all about.

There were Kings and Queens in Africa;
today young black men are more concerned with money,
cars and jewelry,
and sistas with their hair and nails all done; having a child
out of wedlock is a common thing.
Marriage and family don't mean anything.

God, I need you to work this out!

When my father found out my mother was pregnant, he disappeared.

This left two children fatherless, with holes in our hearts, when my twin sister and I were born. It's wasn't just an absence of my father in the photo album, it was an absence in my life that cut deep into my soul. The results went deep, deeper than the eye could see. I didn't feel whole; there was something missing. As a child, I could not put my feelings into thoughts, but I somehow knew it was brokenness.

As a teen and young adult, I made the wrong decisions; I kept doing the things that led to nowhere, and at times, became the things no one wants to become. Most were my efforts to fill in the emptiness left from my father's absence.

While growing up, I didn't see myself as a bad kid. I was more mischievous than anything, and that got me into a lot of trouble and set me on the wrong path. My mother and stepfather raised me in a middle-class town. On the outside, everything looked good. But over time, not having my biological father around and living with a stepfather who drank daily, was too hard to process. In the 7th grade, I started stealing from my stepfather's marijuana stash. Trouble soon followed. After being caught at school with a marijuana joint, I was expelled and sent to an alternative school.

By 16, I had discovered alcohol, started drinking heavily and also began selling cocaine. By 17, I was doing cocaine; selling it was no longer good enough. By this time, I was also bouncing from girl to girl. My senior year, I missed 64 days of school but still graduated because my grades were good. I didn't need to do these things for money, but I felt power, felt like a man.

The next year I went off to college at Virginia State University. The reality: I was a full-time drug dealer and part-time college student with a minor in chasing women. While at school, I got a call from a girl I had previously been involved with; she was pregnant. In addition to becoming a father, I was about to have two other life changing events.

THE COCAINE SEIZURE AND A PRAYER

After a long night of partying, I went into a cocaine seizure. My life was passing before my eyes. I don't remember everything, but I remember thinking that I might die, that this might be the end. At my worst moment, I cried out to the only one that could help me. I cried out to God. I had always believed in God, but the reality was I didn't care about God on a regular basis, however, something instinctively compelled me to cry out to Him.

I cried out and promised God that if He would save me from death, I would never do cocaine again. He heard and answered my prayer and I lived. I also ended my cocaine use that day. I believe He broke the habit and desire I had for cocaine. Two miracles! I lived, and I gave up cocaine all in one night and through one prayer.

I was serious about leaving the drug dealer and cocaine using life, so I made one last delivery and cleaned out my house of all drugs. I thought that stage of my life was over, but it was still following me.

During my sophomore year, when I was 19, my house was raided, and I went to jail for 3 months. I thank God that I had cleaned out the drugs so that I did not go away for an extended period of time, but they still found things that enabled them to put me in jail for a few months.

All of this by 19. Not exactly my goals of what I wanted to be while I was growing up! I spent my 20th birthday in jail trying to figure out what I would do with my life. I also made a vow that I would never go back to jail.

I stuck to my vow of never doing cocaine again, and also never selling drugs again, but I still regularly medicated my pain through weed, women and wine. My son was also born while I was in jail. I still remember his mother telling me to get my act together because I had a son to raise. I took that seriously even though I knew I would never be with her.

MARRIAGE WILL FIX THINGS!

Even though some things had gone the wrong way, there were still some things going in the right direction. I figured that marriage was a good thing and that would help me and also make me happy. At age 26, I married but unfortunately, I did not know how to treat a wife and still didn't know what real love was. With all that I did see, there were no healthy role models to help me emulate or help me understand how a husband should treat a wife. Honestly, I really didn't know how to have a healthy relationship with anyone! I got married on August 24th and met my mistress on October 4th, both in the same year. She had her own house, and many days, after kissing my wife good bye, I would head straight to my mistress's house for the day. I was the product of one of my father's multiple relationships that produced five children in a 2½ year span. I was walking *in my father's shoes.*

Within four years, I was divorced. I was another statistic. In that same time, my best friend was murdered, my grandmother and uncle died, and my life was spinning out of control. My life had no foundation to build on. I kept building pretty things but every time a storm came, my beautiful little houses would get washed away. It was very frustrating! How come all my efforts end up like beautiful sinking ships?

I thought I was the man, but in reality, I was leaving emotional casualties everywhere I went and I was damaging and causing myself great sorrow. This cycle of multiple women continued, resulting in six abortions and a miscarriage. I had been judging my father about having eight children by six women, and I was very mad at him. When I thought about it, the reality hit me that the only difference between us was that his children were alive and mine had been aborted. I was walking *in my father's shoes.*

STUMBLING FORWARD

Not knowing what else to do, I just kept going. I hadn't learned yet that I could press pause on life, you know, take a time out to adjust my game plan, so I just kept doing the same things. In some ways, life got better as I started a mortgage company and a construction company. The money flowed in and the lifestyle got more expensive. I was living the life that others only dreamt about: fine wine, $1,500 bottles of Louis 13th scotch, the best cars, and all the other material trappings. But the missing pieces of my life always came back to sabotage the good things I was doing. At age 36, I was arrested with a D.U.I. and found myself back in a jail cell, the very thing I had vowed I would never let happen again. That night was the beginning of the real change I needed to make that got me where I am today. We'll get back to that, but first, let's look at how my brokenness began as a little boy.

KICKED OUT OF SCHOOL IN THE 7TH GRADE

So, in the 7th grade, I was caught with a joint and kicked out of school and sent to an alternate school for troubled kids. This was when I started becoming a statistic. Here are just a few of the type of statistics, most of which I have lived.

- Nationally, 15.3 percent of children living with a never-married mother and 10.7 percent of children living with a divorced mother have been expelled or suspended from school, compared to only 4.4 percent of children living with both biological parents.[7]

- 75% of adolescent patients in chemical abuse centers come from fatherless homes.[8]

I started smoking weed at age 12 and abused drugs and alcohol for 20 years. I not only didn't have my dad around to teach me to not use drugs, I actually used to steal weed from my stepfather's stash as I grew up.

- Fatherless boys and girls are: twice as likely to drop out of high school; twice as likely to end up in jail; four times more likely to need help for emotional or behavioral problems.[9]

I spent 90 days in jail for being involved in fraudulent activities, which could have been longer, however I was in college and the judge was very lenient. I had actually cleaned out my house of drugs after my cocaine seizure, which saved me years in jail!

I also had a lot of anger problems growing up, some that even led to physical violence against women. Most men would say they would never want to hurt or be aggressive towards a woman but my reality was that I had so much anger stored within me that it came out. This often happens to innocent women whose men grew up without fathers. Yes, all men are capable of this, and yes men from all backgrounds can be abusive, but we have to deal with the reality of this elevated behavior in men without a father in the household. Abuse is never acceptable but we have to name the sickness to begin to heal the sickness! The statistics continue...

- 71% of pregnant teenagers lack a father.[10]

- In a study of 700 adolescents, researchers found that "compared to families with two natural parents living in the home, adolescents from single-parent families have been found to engage in greater and earlier sexual activity." [11]

No one likes to ever think of themselves as a statistic, but my life matches up with these trends and statistics. I became sexually active at around 14 and I had my son at 19 years old. These statistics are not just people's opinions, these are confirmed through behavioral science and government statistical processes. In other words, they are harsh realities that must be dealt with if they are ever going to change. These things are damaging and cause huge amounts of confusion in people's lives.

I BECAME THE MAN I NEVER MET

I didn't meet my father until I was 24 years old, but make no mistake, I had become the man I never met. Were these things hardwired in me or did I learn them? I think the answer is both.

HARDWIRED

Some things I did not choose, and no one influenced. Science would call it genes or genetic predisposition. My height, my build, my smile… those were genetic. Even my personality. Just like my dad, I was a lady's man. Attracting and conquering the next woman was never a problem. In fact, it was so easy, so many times, it became a problem!

I was good with my hands; I could paint rooms and houses and build things. I could have chosen to be a contractor if I wanted to, but I wanted more money and preferred to use my brain to make my living! But later on, I found out my dad was good with his hands. We even had a construction business together for a season.

I was smooth. I knew how to get my way just like my dad. I don't know if you would call it a gift or a talent, but it was there, no doubt. Many nights, I would set myself up at the end of the bar, with a bottle of champagne and guarantee you it was a matter of time until I was approached by a beautiful young lady. It was one of the games I played, and I always won!

THINGS LEARNED

Other things I learned along the way, and many made how I was hard-wired even worse. I learned about alcohol and drugs. For all the negative things my dad did, he was never a drinker or used drugs. Maybe it was my environment, the times and the availability. Drugs were there for my pleasure, for great personal profit and gave me a lot of power to do and get what I wanted. My father learned to escape the responsibility of being a father by abandoning his children. I learned to escape responsibility through abortion. On one hand, I took total responsibility for my son London, but for 6 other children, I either directly or through my absence encouraged their abortion. Maybe I just used another tool to achieve the same thing.

Many of these statistics are clear cut and easy to understand. Others can be strange and very awkward to actually live. Let me share some of the weirdness that my family experienced that goes beyond mere numbers and simple consequences of bad behavior.

MY HALF SISTER'S DAUGHTER AND CHAOS OF MY SIBLINGS

One of my biological sisters by another woman than my mom, had a fear that if her daughter started dating, she could actually start dating one of her brothers from the same father. Five of my father's eight children lived in northern New Jersey, which led to many of us being connected in some way. With multiple children from the same father running around in the same county and even the same town, over time, we started meeting our own biological half-brothers and sisters. It wasn't until my father's funeral that we all were actually together in the same place for the first time.

This type of thing causes a child and even adults to have questions. Some of them make a person question not only their identity, but also their personal worth. Life and human value can become cheapened. You don't feel valuable enough for your dad to stick around, and then you meet many others that were not valued so at some point you ask, "Who is valuable"?

LIFE GETS CHEAPENED

A type of cycle can start going on in your thought process. You can start thinking that if you're not valuable, then nobody is. If nobody is valuable, then what happens to them or you doesn't really matter. Sex, drugs, alcohol and all the games make sense because life is not about valuing people, it's just about having fun, the next thrill or worse, proving you are valuable at the expense of others.

When human worth is devalued, what you do to yourself or someone else really doesn't matter. It's the environment to become a statistic. You flow with the currents that flow around you. If it's alcohol, you do that. If it's pot, you do that. If girls are the measure of success, you treat sex with them like making a clutch basket in a pick-up game instead of a human being. It's almost like gravity pulls you in these directions without a stronger force of a father pulling you in a better direction. I've seen this happen in my life, my friends and even entire streets and neighborhoods, this can be the norm. Money by itself is not the solution either. I grew up in a middle-class home and neighborhood. From the outside, I had everything a young man could ever want. Two parents in the house who worked hard and provided me with what I needed. The problem was my emotional and spiritual brokenness were stronger than the fact that my parents had money.

STRANGE CONNECTIONS STARTED TO POP UP

In 1995 my twin sister worked as a teacher and had a student that always told her that she just looked like her mom. She also kept telling her mom that she looked like her teacher. Ten years later, she learned that the little girl was her biological niece because her student's mom had the same father, my father. This can mess with a child's mind. Children thrive in situations that are stable and safe. Not knowing who you are related to and having no one to help you navigate these things can be very unnerving. A parent's job is to provide a safe atmosphere for a child to grow and thrive. It gets more complicated.

I had a best friend whose mother had a boyfriend, who's best friend was a guy name Willie and we called him Chill-Will. Chill-Will turned out to be my uncle. I had known Chill-Will for 2 years before I found my father. It was very emotional for both of us when we found out we were related because we would always talk about life and he was really cool. There's more. As time went on, and it even continues to this day, there is always more.

Three of my brothers and sisters went to school with someone my twin sister and I were acquainted with. One of my other sisters went to high school with my best friend from college. Another one of my sisters went to school with one of my ex-girlfriends. One of my brothers went to school with my cousin and they were really close and didn't know we were related. My father knew many of my friend's parents from the neighborhoods but they didn't know he was my father.

At some point, my siblings and I were concerned that we either did or could have had sex with each other. Thankfully, this never happened, but some of us were in the same age range and were local enough that this was possible. Once again, instead of having a sense of clarity, identity and purpose, this was just a hot mess of confusion that made life seem unsafe. These are some of the reasons that drugs and alcohol become the go to in order to escape from reality on many different levels.

CHAPTER 5

IN A LITTLE BOY'S MIND

God took the strength of a mountain,
the majesty of a tree,
the warmth of a summer sun,
the calm of the quiet sea,

The generous soul of nature,
The comforting arm of night,
The wisdom of the ages,
The power of the eagles flight,
The joy of a morning in spring,

The faith of a mustard seed,
The patience of eternity,
the depth of family need,
Then God combined these qualities.

When there was nothing more to add,
He knew his masterpiece was complete,
And so,
He Called it......DAD[12]

I often laid in bed wondering where my dad was. Why isn't he with me? Why doesn't he want me? Why did he leave? Who is he? What is he like? My mother often told me I was just like my father. When I did good, I was just like him, and when I did wrong, I was just like him. I often thought, "Who is this man that I am just like?" How was I supposed to be like him when he's wasn't there to show me how? These unanswered questions resulted in unresolved anger and shaky foundation as I attempted to build my life. I wanted a dad to play catch with and to help teach me to be strong. Without him, I often turned to my friends who were in the same situation. I knew there were some things wrong with my dad since he wasn't around. I also instinctively knew that there were good things about my dad, things I needed.

THE GOOD SIDE OF MY DAD

My dad was tall, dark, handsome and as smooth as they come. A few choice words and a look were all it took, most of the time, to get a young lady's attention. In many ways, my dad was irresistible and a magnet for women. He was the life of the party and someone people wanted to be around. As I grew, and my mother recognized my physical features, I think it brought her both pride and pain as I grew to be more like my father. As a young man, it wasn't long before I began to learn how girls liked me too and with a few words and a look, I knew I was in control; I was just like my dad.

I later found out how generous my dad was. He would give you the shirt off his back and help anyone in need. Deep down, he had a good heart, but it was a heart that I would never know as a child. Later in his life, his church gave him an award for his servanthood and generosity towards others. I found out about many of these good characteristics later in life, but as a little boy, there were mostly gaps and question marks.

THE DARK SIDE OF MY DAD AND HOW IT HURT A LITTLE BOY

My dad was notorious for being able to get women in bed, but when they got pregnant, he disappeared. For my mom, he was her first physical relationship and disappeared when my mom told him she was pregnant with me and my twin sister. It would be years before any contact would be had again. This was the pattern as my father had 8 children by six women in a 20-year time frame.

I followed in his footsteps, having my first child by the time I was 19. Determined to not have children all over the place, like my dad, I discovered a modern way called abortion that wasn't as available or socially acceptable in my dad's day. It wasn't long before I looked back and could count six abortions that I knew about and had encouraged. I may not have repeated having as many children as my father, but in many ways, I feel I did something worse to both the children and the women whom I impregnated. Abortion may be a quick solution, but the regret stays with you. Many women experience depression, increased alcohol and drug use and even PTSD after abortion.[13] Men often go through depression, but also become more callous as they shut down emotionally. Deep down, they know that they both began and ended a life through their actions or inactions. I often turned to drugs or alcohol to mask the pain, and to the next woman to make me feel important as I repeated the same mistakes.

IDENTITY CRISIS AND THE PAIN IT CAUSED

After reuniting with my dad and trying to figure out who this man was, I asked him, "Who are you?" My father, 70 years old at the time, sat back in the seat, took a breath and said, "I don't know," and all the pain left me. You see, I had been wrestling with the same question, "Who am I?" Just like my dad, I wrestled. I defined myself by the women I slept with, the respect people gave me and countless temporary successes. I also defined myself by my failures that seemed to gnaw at my soul, and at times, make me not like myself. God's Word teaches that "the truth will set you free" (John 8:32). That day, I lived that verse as my father humbly admitted that he did not know who he was.

I could finally stop seeking an answer from a man who did not have one. This also explained, on some level, why he had done so many things. But there was freedom. I did not have to keep wondering, looking or searching. The final answer – there is no answer. I could finally stop wondering. After 70 years of bold living, my father still had no clue who he was. This also set me free, because I could stop striving to be someone, something that that was a mystery, that didn't exist. I didn't have to live up to some standard because there was no standard. I had to look to a new standard. I had already begun learning about a standard that God had set for me. It was a good standard. It was something I could do because God would help me. Where my father had no standard and was unable to help me, I continued to learn how to walk in my heavenly Father's standards. I also realized that my heavenly Father is never absent. He is always present, always loving and always there. These truths continue to set me free.

SELFISH

My father's decision to neglect me was incredibly selfish. He chose to enjoy the pleasures of a physical relationship with my mom and forego responsibility for the children that relationship produced. He did this to all his children. His brokenness broke a little boy. A little boy should have his father there to hug him, play with him, to make him feel safe and valuable. Because my dad didn't value me, I wrestled with my self-worth. I thought maybe it was my fault or that I was not good enough. Reading this, you may think my conclusions were obviously wrong, but in a little boy's mind, what other conclusions can you come up with? The reality: I was not important enough in my dad's mind for him to be around.

I thank God for my mom; she did a great job teaching me to value myself, but the reality is, certain things need to come from a father in the same way that only certain things can come from a mother. A boy defines himself by his father; there is just a natural instinct to do that. A fatherless boy has no alternative to begin to look for something else to define himself by.

SELF-CENTERED AND SELF-ABSORBED

When you define yourself by your conquests, all you care about is yourself, and you devalue others. My father lacked conviction; he didn't care that he was hurting these women and the children he was producing. He only cared about himself. His only commitment was to enjoy life and not let anything else get in the way. I too became that person as I walked *in my father's shoes.*

MANIPULATOR

My father always worked to get his way. Whether it was with women or with a job, he was always looking for an angle. He was able to come across as a friend and someone who cared. It was confusing. He would give you the shirt off his back and help people in so many ways. Then when it was time, he always made sure he got his!

He was a complicated man! So much good, but then undermined by deceit. That was the picture of my life until I was in my mid 30s. It's what the world teaches us. It's what the streets teach us. When we are driven by our desires and our insecurities, it becomes our default mechanism, or go-to technique to get what we want. For some, it's like gravity pulling us to win in life, by any means necessary. With my dad, it was a well-developed art form. As a child, he wasn't around because being around meant sacrificing personal desires to be there for someone else. That is what a husbands and fathers do. They sacrifice themselves for the benefit of others. My father never learned that lesson and paid a deep price for, missing out, not only on the lives of his children, but never really getting what he was looking for.

NO INTEGRITY

Integrity means that you are the same person all the time in every situation. Basically, that you are who you are. My dad, like so many other people, was a different person based on the situation. This is so important to kids growing up. Knowing that their father is dependable and consistent creates inner peace and a feeling of safety. When that is not present, there is insecurity and an urge for protection, guidance and relationship. This is why young boys will gravitate towards a coach or a gang leader, or a young lady will run to a boy, in an attempt to meet those needs. Whoever seems to be the best person they can find, usually gets their loyalty. This is why so many people and their relationships are not healthy.

As I became more like my dad, I saw how the lack of integrity was damaging to both my life and to the people I was connected to. Integrity must be learned. Without it, many of our best efforts are often sabotaged by our actions. I have spent the last 10 years of my life learning how to be a man of integrity.

LIAR

My father was a liar. Hate to say it, but he was a straight up liar. He could look you in the face and with a smile on his face, he would lie, lie, lie. When I met him, he told me he was a millionaire. Later, he showed up on my door step with no place to live, then he lied to not have to pay me an agreed upon amount for rent. One day, one of my brothers came into the house and started an argument with me because he said I took the money out of my father's mattress. There was never any money.

He told my in-laws about all the properties he owned. The only dirt that man owned was the dirt on his shoes! He could sweet talk and lie like no other man I ever met. I picked up that skill, too. I had no problem buying girls drinks, telling them how special they were, and even telling them I loved them...while still at the bar! Men lie because it often works. My father could have won an Oscar for some of the lies he told. He was good at it. Even though he really did change his life in so many ways, he never did beat that habit of lying.

THE SILENCE OF ABSENCE

There is a quiet that is not good in a little boy's mind when his dad is not around. Instead of the noise of laughter, playing catch and your dad watching you play ball growing up, there is a silence. Let me be clear, the silence is wrong. It's not supposed to be there. There is a loneliness to that silence because the person who is supposed to fill that gap simply isn't there. My father's absence was not only silence, but pain. Like someone who has hunger pains because they need food. But for me, those hunger pains were never met as a child, teen, or young adult. I had to learn to navigate life with a starving soul, one my father never fed.

MY SHIP HAD NO CAPTAIN

A ship without a captain (be it good or bad) cannot sail.[14]

-LEON FOSTER THOMAS

Every ship has a captain for two reasons. First, to get to the proper destination in the right amount of time. Secondly, to navigate any storms along the way. Without a father to guide me, I found myself living life void of goals, lacking direction. I was also not equipped when it came time to make choices and to navigate storms and failures which compounded over time and left me like a ship floating in the sea without a compass to set my path. This also left me seeking other guidance from men who had similar experiences and lacked the same things I did. The blind leading the blind.

THE PROPER DESTINATION

Imagine a ship trying to cross the ocean without any plan. No maps, no compass, no destination and no one who could read the stars. You're probably thinking that would be pretty dumb. You'd be right, and no one would knowingly sail across the sea without a destination and the knowledge and tools to navigate a vast ocean. But I was trying to navigate the vast ocean of childhood, teen, and young adult years with no real destination, few navigational tools and no captain steering the boat called life. On a ship, the captain's job is to ensure the safety of all his passengers, even if it means he dies. There is a rule that the captain goes down with the ship unless everyone else gets off first. For the captain, saving the passengers on his ship is life or death. That's the type of commitment a ship's captain is supposed to have. That's the type of commitment a father is supposed to have for his children.

Getting to the proper destination... First, growing up, I had no idea what I was aiming for. "Success" sure, "popularity" sure, but what does that really mean, and according to whose standard? I sure can't tell you what the proper destination was growing up, but I can tell you what it wasn't! Getting kicked out of school for pot in the 7th grade – not the right destination. Impregnating a woman I worked with at 18 years old – naah. Begging God to spare my life in the middle of a cocaine seizure where I thought my heart may explode, not getting any closer to that perfect destination!

You see, you would NEVER sail a ship without a captain. But I found myself trying to navigate life with no captain. The other thing I came to realize was that you can never reach a destination that you are not trying to get to! In life you can do a lot of things, even do a lot of good things, but without a destination, your trip can never be successful.

I WAS MISSING 2 CAPTAINS

Having an absentee father left a huge gap in my life. But, there was another Captain who could have helped me; which I didn't really understand until much later in my life. The other Captain I could have had was God. It's not that He wasn't there for me. It was a combination of me wanting to do what I wanted to do and the reality that I did not understand God.

It's kind of funny because I always went to church. For many years, I was committed to church and went every week, but I wasn't committed to God! Part of God's plan is to lead us through life. You see, it started with my dad not being led by God. Instead, he was really led by his flesh. His whole life was controlled by what his mind and body wanted. Without God, we are like little kids set free in a candy store, allowed to eat anything we want. With too much freedom, too much desire and no direction it often equals disaster. That was my dad's life. Since he lived a life very distant from God, he could not be the father I needed him to be. He did not live out true purpose in this area of his life. His absence and lack of God knowledge made it impossible for him to teach me about God.

As a result, I grew up with a distorted view of God. I saw Him as judgmental and someone I could never please. I lived my life knowing I was doing things I knew were not pleasing to God, but I had no power to stop myself. I also had trouble thinking of a "heavenly father" since I had no earthly father as an example. It's not that I would not have let God lead my life, I just couldn't picture a heavenly Father who really cared, especially since life had shown me that I wasn't important enough for my own father to lead me through life.

THE STORMS

Then, there are the storms that we all face and have to navigate. When you don't navigate life well, the storms get more intense and last much longer than they need to last! What should be a stubbed toe becomes a broken leg. Unmet loneliness or insecurities, that all people face, become wrong relationships and alcohol or drug habits. Ships at sea do all they can to avoid storms, and if they get caught in one, they try to navigate out of it and into calm waters as soon as possible. Other times, ships make a wrong turn and something that could have been a short encounter can become days stuck in a storm causing huge damage, sea sickness and even sinking of the ship. I truly believe a strong father would have helped me make more right choices and navigate life's tough issues in a better way.

MY LOST FRIENDS HELPED ME GET MORE LOST

Most of my friends were in the same boat as me. Imagine a bunch of overly hormonal boys with no guidance and no one to guide them through life, trying to lead each other. This was a bad look! No one knew how to navigate life, so we were led by our brokenness and desires. It was like giving a bunch of kids matches and telling them not to play with fire! We spent many years burning things down. We burned down our own lives and the girls we used who were also lonely with no dads. When everyone is going in the wrong direction, wrong suddenly seems like what you're supposed to do.

Without my dad to steer me in the right direction, there were a lot of times I took a wrong turn and just kept on going. Most kids don't like discipline and correction, but I wish my dad was around to discipline and correct me. That's one way dad's help steer the ship of their children's lives. Unfortunately, my dad didn't have that discipline growing up, making it almost impossible for him to know how to do that for me. This made my life a lot tougher than it needed to be.

MY CHOICES MADE THINGS WORSE

My own choices made life even harder. I was like that kid released in the candy store with no rules. I was out of control, and living without limits, partying and women led me to some terrible places. It also created a lifestyle of chaos. One storm led to another until my life was a never-ending series of storms. Honestly, I enjoyed a lot of the drama, at least for a season, until I came to the end of myself. It's funny, when I came to the end of myself, it was like I came to the beginning of God. When I really connected with God, I found out He was a lot better than I ever imagined; He was the One I needed.

First, I learned He had always been there and was waiting for me with open arms. I also learned He was not angry with me, me even after all I did to myself and to others. He simply wanted to meet me where I was and help me go forward. I realized that even though I could not depend on my earthly father, I could depend on my heavenly Father. This helped me because I needed someone to depend on and over time, even though I hoped to connect with my father and that he would be there for me, I came to realize I needed to move forward whether or not my father would ever be there for me. When I truly surrendered leadership of my life to Jesus, He began to lead me down the path I was meant to travel. Some things changed overnight, and other things are still changing. Even though I am far from perfect, I know each day my heavenly Father is there to lead me. It's a journey, but I have found that journeying with God is much different and better than journeying alone.

SECTION 2

College and Young Adulthood

CHAPTER 7

IDENTITY CRISIS

*Many of us will not realize who we are because
we do not believe in ourselves.*[15]

- SUNDAY ADELAJZ

How we view ourselves sets the direction of our lives. If we see ourselves as valuable and successful, we will live a certain way. If we see ourselves as worthless and only capable of failure, we will live a completely different way. Most of us wrestle somewhere in the middle. Growing up, and even as an adult, I've had to fight to learn who I truly am.

Being continually told I was just like my father resulted in more questions than answers. Bottom line, I didn't know my self-identity or who I was really supposed to be. Since my dad was not there to direct me or tell me who I really was, I continued my journey letting society define me. Our culture told me if I did well with the girls, had money, and did well in sports, I was valuable. So I played ball, sold drugs, started businesses and made sure I had the finest woman on my arm when I walked in the club, and I drove the best cars. The problem was no matter how much people were impressed, all these worldly accomplishments still left me empty inside.

As I said in an earlier chapter, one of the things that helped me forgive my father was when I asked him who he really was, and he said, "I don't know." It helped me because I had a picture in my mind of who he was supposed to be. I was very angry because he did not live up to that picture. I found a level of freedom when I understood that in some ways he could never live up to the picture I had because he literally had no idea about who he was. He also had no target to aim for, no goal for real manhood. Growing up, I was walking in those same shoes. I had no idea who I was or that I was becoming someone, whoever that was. I was just living day by day and doing the best I knew how to do.

WHERE DOES IDENTITY COME FROM?

Identity comes from two main sources. The first is from God and the second is your parents and family. I lacked both main sources in the sense that I was living a life that was disconnected from God, and my father was absent, so I lacked his guidance and direction both in the natural and the spiritual. Yes, I had my mom and she did a very good job. But neither my mom, nor my step-dad could fill the gap caused by my father's absence. I often rebelled against my stepfather screaming, "You're not my dad!" Many young men suffer from this gap. My step-dad was also physically and verbally abusive, which made things even more confusing. I was angry and powerless to confront this grown man who belittled me and drove me to further wrestle with my self-identity. So, I struggled forward with a smile on my face and a strong body, but I was broken inside.

IDENTITY FIRST COMES FROM GOD

First and foremost, we are created in God's image:

So God created mankind in his own image, in the image of God he created them; male and female he created them. -GENESIS 1:27

This was a revolutionary thought in my head. I probably really didn't understand this until about 37 years old. Once I got it, it redefined my life and where I was going. It put me on a different path. I had been living my life in a below-standard type of way. I was walking a dirty, broken path instead of a healthy, prosperous path because I was not aiming for the high standards that God had already pre-wired and pre-determined me to live! My target identity had been defined by the Hip Hop culture and a bunch of unfocused, testosterone driven, weed smoking peers. Oh yeah – I was not just one of the bunch, I was often the leader. Being created in God's image means we are meant to think and live a certain way. This speaks of purpose. Many people have confused a list of religious rules for a God-given purpose and plan for our lives. I had settled for man's religion, which was a poor substitute for a personal relationship with God.

BEYOND CHURCH AND "BELIEVING IN GOD"

Keep in mind, I believed in God and went to church during all of my bad decisions and even criminal activities. But to truly tap into God, I had to be willing to submit my life to His leadership. Once I did that, He began to transform me into His image in the way I thought, acted and treated people. He began to guide, shape, and mold me.

Many people don't like the idea of "submitting" to God or anyone else. It drives their minds to think of oppressive and legalistic religious systems that try to control them. I found out that this is not what the Bible or Christianity is really about. It's about having a loving God who directs us and becomes our source. The reality is that someone or something leads us and controls us. I have spoken to many men who get high, drunk and sleep around with many women, claiming to be free, but in reality, they are controlled by their need for the next high. Trust me, I lived this for years and it is very controlling. I found out that serving God is the only way to freedom, especially from the things that I thought made me free but really controlled my existence.

GOD BECAME MY GPS SYSTEM

Remember the days before Google Maps and GPS systems? We had maps, printed out MapQuest directions and don't forget the favorite... we stopped at gas stations hoping the guy pumping gas could tell us where to go! Don't forget the favorite of many men. They just drove around lost and pretended like they knew where they were going.

This was my life for decades' I just drove around lost. Don't get me wrong, I had a lot of fun along the way, like a bunch of college kids on a road trip with no plan. It could be fun, but it doesn't get you anywhere, or most often, it gets you to a place you don't want to be. I let my flesh and my peers lead me wherever, no questions asked.

Over time, I learned to let God define my identity and lead me in all areas of my life. When GPS first came out, it was revolutionary. When I began to follow God's leading, it was life changing! The whole game changed. It was like a losing team bringing in a winning coach and turning the whole program around.

But for a GPS to work, you have to pull it out of the glove compartment, plug it in and actually listen and do what it tells you to do. It's not enough to "believe in" the fact that a GPS works, you have to put it to work. I remember people actually arguing with GPS systems – literally! They didn't like the direction it sent them or thought they knew better. Some people just don't want to be told what to do. While GPS is not perfect, God is perfect. Once I locked in and focused on God, I let Him begin to tell me who I am and where I should go. Today, I am a CEO, former Vice-President of a national men's ministry, have a master's degree, and am a faithful husband to a beautiful wife because I began to let Him tell me who I am. I am God's child, created in God's image to live out an amazing purpose. Without self-identifying as God's child and living it out, I would not have experienced and lived any of these great things.

SELF-IDENTITY AND FAMILY

Family is also a huge factor in creating self-identity. Parent's words shape and mold children. If parents tell their child they are valuable, smart and have a great future, they think about themselves that way. Many times, rich people tell and teach their kids to be rich, and they grow up rich. Many poor people think poor, act poor, and poverty is transferred to the next generation. While this is not always the case, we can look around to see many examples of this.

The statistics are astounding in terms of repeat behaviors and bad choices that are made that either repeat a parent's actions or happen in increased percentages in children growing up without a father in the household. These include depression, criminal activity, children born out of wedlock, broken marriages, jail, etc.

So, my self-identity from my family was greatly defined by an absent father, an abusive alcoholic step-father and my teenage peers. Not an ideal situation! Yes, my mother had a good influence on me and even my step-father helped me in many ways, but they did not fill many gaps. Both my mom and step-dad had good jobs and provided for me greatly, but these things did not meet my spiritual and emotional needs. There are many needs that money can't meet. In many ways, money just let me sin in better style.

DEFINING SIN

Most people cringe when they hear the word "sin". It paints an image of a self-righteous mean old man telling people not to do anything fun – ever. But that's not what the word means. My pastor, Dr. David Ireland has explained it many times. "Sin" is an old English word that means "missing the mark, it was a term to describe an archer who shot an arrow and missed the target." Thanks, Pastor Dave! Sin basically means doing anything outside of God's will for your life that will essentially hurt you, others, or keep you from your purpose. Sin is more directional than just an action.

Growing up, many forces pushed me in the wrong direction. They encouraged me to "miss the mark" in my life. Many people will look at my drinking, drugging, lying and sleeping around as "the sin" but they were only actions that resulted from my wrong self-identity and lack of purpose.

God didn't give me an amazing wife, a great career etc. because I decided to stop cussing and smoking weed, He simply guided me to the things that he had already prepared and had waiting for me. It was when I redefined my identity as a child of God that I was able to walk the path I was supposed to be on. If I never made that decision, I would have stayed on the broken and painful path that life had put me on.

OVERCOMING MY DAD'S SIN

As I said before, "sin" basically means taking the wrong path and committing wrong actions. In many ways, my father's absence was setting me up for failure in many ways. His absence also left me more susceptible to the traps of this world, and I was often more than eager to take a bite of that cheese! So many people pay the price for their parents' faults and failures, but people don't have to.

Yes, what our parents do can either give us an advantage or make life more difficult, but we never have to be defined by our parents' failures or short comings. Once I connected with God and my understanding changed, I got to work. I went back and finished my undergraduate degree and then went on to obtain a master's degree in organizational leadership, which paved the way for me to become a CEO of a counseling clinic that helps hundreds of people every week.

I also had the support of my amazing wife who would have never gotten involved with me before I became a Christian because of the way I lived. When we understand who we are and start walking it out, our entire life can change. For me, it all began when I allowed God to show me who I really was and began surrounding myself with people who were good for me.

CHAPTER 8

MY FLESH WAS MY KING

Those who live according to the flesh have their minds set on what
the flesh desires; but those who live in accordance with the Spirit
have their minds set on what the Spirit desires. The mind
governed by the flesh is death, but the mind governed
by the Spirit is life and peace.
-ROMANS 8:5-6

I lived my life trying to satisfy desires that only grew when I fed them. One beautiful woman wasn't enough, neither was a pile of money or many accomplishments. The flesh always wants more, and this leads to death. My emotions, conscience and even passion for life died. I needed drugs, alcohol or sex to medicate the pain and slow emotional and spiritual death I was living. For many years, I was still very distant from God's life-giving Spirit. Inner peace was unimaginable until I connected with God.

The difference between humans and animals is that animals are driven by instinct, and at times, uncontrollable desires instead of intellectual, emotional and spiritual guidance. But for 37 years, my actions were driven by what my flesh desired, whether it be survival or simply the next thrill. I was consumed by physical pleasure of drugs, sex and alcohol. Over time the intensity grew but the satisfaction decreased. I lived fast and furious, but I was going nowhere. Though I was highly intelligent, I was living more like an animal than a man. I was giving myself everything my physical body desired, but I was dead spiritually and my emotional life was a train wreck on the inside even though the outside looked great.

THERE IS A DIFFERENCE

There is a huge difference between people and animals. God created both, but people were created in His image:

So God created mankind in his own image, in the image of God he created them; male and female he created them. -GENESIS 1:27

Animals were created for people to enjoy and also for work and food. People were created for God to be in relationship with Him. Our brains, emotions and ability to choose things are on a totally different level. Animals are hardwired to live by instinct and physical urges. Yes, humans have instincts and urges, but we have the ability to choose how we react to them. Our emotions and urges are meant to be blessings designed to drive us to achieve amazing things and build great relationships, not to rule us and destroy us slowly or in a disastrous way.

No one would think it would be normal for a human to fight and kill a person over a ham and cheese sandwich or rape a woman in broad daylight, but these sort of things like killing your competition over food, or forceful sex, in the animal world would be normal, but both illegal and immoral for humans. So, we don't take it to these extremes, but many men live like animals, unable to control themselves in their anger or sexuality. They live like animals who must have and conquer women rather than be focused on commitment and faithfulness to one amazing relationship. In a sense, we trade our exceptional place in creation for something less.

LIVING LIKE A DOG

It's funny how we use certain words. Yes, we use the word "dog" as a simple word to acknowledge our friends and don't mean anything about it, but let's look at some culture behind it. When it comes to sex, dogs have sex when the female dog, which is literally called a "bitch" in dog breeder's language, is in heat. The male dog has sex and then simply walks away. He is ready at any time and just looking for the female dog that is in the right mood and season, so it is quick, easy and no strings attached.

Isn't it funny how many guys who run around calling each other "dog" are looking for lonely women, aka those horny and willing to have sex, so that they can have sex and just walk away? They call them bitches, treat them like bitches and call themselves dogs. Maybe I am making too much about words, maybe not. But words are powerful and even unintentionally, we become what we think and speak.

LIFE GETS CHEAPENED

In this scenario, women totally get cheapened. They become a piece of meat. They may be a 99-cent cheeseburger or $100 steak, but at the end of the day, they become a piece of meat to be consumed. In addition to the cheapening of women and relationships, men are also cheapened. It's funny how when women sleep around, they are seen as less valuable, but men are seen as more valuable when they sleep around. This is often the picture our culture paints, but reality is much different. Men also are cheapened because they, too, become common.

Yes, I painted the picture of the traditional male dominated scenario, but things are changing, and women are playing the same games men play. So many men are hurt by unfaithful women also. So, the game gets worse.

WINNING ON THE OUTSIDE, LOSING ON THE INSIDE

For me, I looked like I was winning, but on the inside, I was digging an emotional hole. It was like I was spending all my emotions and then some. We understand financial debt, but when we play these games, it's like we create an emotional debt that we can't get out from under. No matter how much we achieve or conquer, the emptiness only grows. The man who has had many women can still walk around with low self-esteem, not much different than the beautiful woman who feels ugly.

SO WE LIE

We lie to ourselves and we lie to others. We tell ourselves how amazing we are, and we try to convince others of the same thing. Each day we lie and tell ourselves we are on the right path. We lie to the next woman. We lie to our boys. We act like we are tough as life eats away at our souls. We mentally replay our escapades like watching a highlight film of our lives and try to convince ourselves that we were great and oh yeah – that means we are still great.

THE GAME ROLLS ON

Unless we call a time out and change the game plan, we will keep playing the same game. In some ways, my father played the same games until he died. He made some changes, but in many ways, he kept playing the only game he knew how to play. The problem is the flesh is never satisfied. We are made up of three parts: body, soul and spirit. God created us in such a way that the spirit would rule the soul and the body, in that order. If we put the body first, it pulls us away from God and ruins our soul, which is our mind and emotions.

The correct pattern is that we are led by God. He directs and builds our spirit-man. When we have that right, God then directs the way we think and feel. This allows us to put our relationships, thoughts and desires in the right places. It allows us to be directed by God and make wise and healthy decisions instead of being driven by unhealthy emotions, which magnify unhealthy dominance of physical desire.

WE HAVE A HUNGER TO FEED

God has given us appetites. One way to look at it is like nutrition. God gives us the desire to eat. When we follow a healthy eating plan, we will be stable and satisfied. When the body has proper nutrition, it is at peace and though it desires more food, its desires are healthy. If we skip breakfast, and don't eat healthy foods, sooner or later we start snacking on junk food and binging. Our normal healthy desires start going to unhealthy or even extreme levels. If we are not being fed spiritually and emotionally, the only thing we have left to feed us is the physical. It's like not eating breakfast and lunch, working hard and then going into a candy store. You will probably eat a lot of unhealthy things.

Since I was emotionally starving and distant from God, I fed myself with alcohol, drugs and women. I've also worked with many men who feed themselves with pornography, greed or many other things. The bottom line is if we don't have the spiritual and emotional things in place, we will live like animals and only feed ourselves in the physical.

EATING FROM THE DUMPSTER

Most people would tell you that they would never eat from a garbage can or dumpster and that sounds right. But the reality is that if someone didn't eat for a couple of days or a week, they would start to dabble in that dumpster. Eventually, they would gladly eat from that dumpster if they are hungry enough.

We just dress up the dumpster and eat things that either we were never supposed to eat, or things that may have been once good, but are now garbage. If the emotional and spiritual gaps are that big, like that starving person, at some point, it's not just a desire but a necessity to eat from that dumpster. The problem with that is it's not healthy. When I lived like an animal, I was eating a lot! But I was still starving on the inside and was destroying myself in both the short and long term.

IT'S A LOSING GAME

Living by the flesh is a losing game. It's like the drug addict trying to satisfy themselves with the next high. It never satisfies, and it never ends. Like a business that doesn't make a profit, it is doomed to go out of business. It's like buying things on credit that you can't afford. You may enjoy the purchases for a season, but I don't know how many people I have spoken to that say the happiness of the purchase doesn't compare to the price of paying it off over time. Living like an animal will get you a season of pleasure and probably notoriety that feels good but isn't worth it in the long run. I played the game hard but at the end of the day, no matter how many "victories" I thought I had, I knew the game I was playing was a losing game.

CHAPTER 9

MEDICATING MY PAIN

My Soul

It all started out as an innocent kiss,
The first time you touched my young LIPS,
I said let me taste just a few sips,

I didn't know how powerful you could be to my young soul,
The control, you would take over my life,
You were my fatal attraction,
I LOVED YOU more that my WIFE,

I got weak every time I looked at you,
the LUST,
the SECRET meetings in the clubs or just sitting in a TUB,

You came to me in so many disguises,
Damn I didn't know you would taste so good,
and even those times when you made my chest burn,
I LOVED you anyway,
Because you made my pain go away,
or (SO I THOUGHT),

even if it was just for a day,
and yet you brought out so much rage from me,
Every time you touched my young lips.

Those sleepless nights when my stomach was turning
And I wished, I didn't have so much of you,
or those times we got into fights together I still wanted more.
You made me feel so good,
You were better than sex to me.
I met you in a bar
And I could sleep with you in my car.

Damn, you had this brotha feening, I just couldn't wait for
Another date so you could touch my young lips.

So, when my pleasure brought me no satisfaction and my failed relationships and business ripped at my soul, I turned to alcohol, drugs and sex to medicate my pain. This poem speaks to the love I had for alcohol. Others turn to pornography or other pursuits to ease the pain of life. It is also amazing how people turn to power, prestige or careers to hide from the pain within. It is amazing to speak to some of the most accomplished men, who are lonely and feel like failures. These things and others may override the pain or at least make us numb for a season, but they don't cure what really ails us. I fully gave myself to many of these things, but at the end of it all, they gave nothing back that lasted.

Pain is a harsh reality of life. I once read that even though love is called the universal language, the true emotion that all people have in common is pain.[16] People go to great lengths to avoid pain, but life has taught me that no matter how fast I run, pain will eventually catch up with me. In fact, pain is often thrust upon us while we are too young to avoid or process this pain. We also feel the pain of others who are in our lives. My pain began when my father walked out on my mother. It continued as I, too, felt my mother's pain of raising two children from a man who ran from his responsibilities. Then there was my mother's reminder that "I was just like my father" which unintentionally reopened the wound caused by his absence.

My pain continued to be felt as a child, teenager and young adult. Like many other young men, I learned that I could either numb my pain through alcohol or drugs or drown it out with the excitement of sex and personal achievement. These things only masked the pain but never healed the root cause. In fact, it wasn't until I was in my mid-thirties that I really began to understand the problem. I think my dad lived his whole life without ever really facing the reality of his own broken soul. One thing I have learned is that if we do not grasp and understand our brokenness, we will never deal with it and will never live the life that God created us to live.

HUNGER PAIN OF THE SOUL

Around the world, many people live with the reality of pain from being physically hungry for food. Millions live throughout the day and lay in bed at night hungry with stomach pains. But there is a type of hunger that is often unseen but is very damaging. For me, I grew up with all the food and physical things I needed, but my soul cried out to be fed by my father.

We often talk about a person being made up of body, mind and soul. Our body is our physical existence, our mind is our intellect, but our soul is our emotions and mental well-being. The reality is that we can be physically strong, intellectually smart, but emotionally damaged and broken. So many people walk around looking great and even doing well academically or in their career but are either empty or hurting in their soul.

GOD CAN RESTORE OUR SOUL

Just like any medical condition or injury, it will often take medical attention and time to heal. Without either one of these, an injury or sickness can grow worse or even become permanent over time. When it comes to healing of the soul, I have realized that Jesus is the great physician! Yes, I believe in counseling. In fact, I am the CEO of the Family Healing Center, which is a counseling center for individuals and families, but no matter how smart we are as people, we are limited. I have great counselors, psychologists, social workers and psychiatrists that work for me, but I have realized that without God healing our wounds, the issues of life will linger and continue to eat away at our souls.

STRONG PEOPLE ARE NOT IMMUNE TO SOUL PAIN

You may or may not be familiar with the Bible but let me give you a little background about a very interesting person. The Bible records the life of a man named David. He was the second king in the nation of Israel. This is the same David that fought and defeated Goliath. He went on to be a mighty warrior who led the army of Israel and fought and won many battles. In today's world, David would be a Navy Seal, Green Beret and a General, all at the same time. He was a man's man and would easily be the strongest and fiercest man we would ever meet. But in Psalm 23, this incredibly strong man is praising God for restoring his broken soul. If David is not immune to having a damaged soul, no man is. It would be almost impossible in this day and age to be as tough as David, but many times throughout the Book of Psalms in the Old Testament, David cries out to God for help after people have betrayed or deserted him, causing pain to his soul. This has helped me as a strong man to know that there are times when I need to cry out to God for help.

Let's take a quick look at Psalm 23 which is one of the most popular chapters in the Bible.

The Lord is my shepherd, I shall not be in want.
He makes me lie down in green pastures, he leads me beside quiet
waters, He restores my soul... -PSALM 23:1-3A

THE LORD IS MY SHEPHERD

This speaks of how God wants to lead, provide for and protect us like a shepherd would take care of his sheep. When the shepherd does his job, the sheep's needs are met. I had to let Jesus lead me, heal me and fill the empty gap in my life left by my natural father. Yes, counseling and strong relationships are helpful but a relationship with Jesus is a supernatural thing that works above and beyond what people can do. It's not either/or, we need both.

HE MAKES ME LIE DOWN IN GREEN PASTURES

This speaks of a couple of things. First, green pastures supply an abundance of food to sheep so they can be satisfied. Secondly, sheep only lie down when they are comfortable and have no fear of danger. One of the things that young people growing up without a father feel is fear. Fear of an emptiness they don't know how to fill. Fear of not being protected and provided for. Fear of not being valuable or worthy of being loved. I learned that God can supernaturally drive these fears away.

HE LEADS ME BESIDE QUIET WATERS

This speaks of God leading us to a peaceful place. Without God, I didn't feel peace. I felt many other things, but peace was not one of them. This is also an issue of the soul. Inner peace demonstrates an absence of fear, anxiety, depression or any of a multitude of feelings. This doesn't mean that we will never feel these things, but when we do feel them, they will come and go because God can give us peace.

In my practice at the Family Healing Center, some people do require medications to deal with these types of issues, but for us, this is a last resort. We also encourage people that do need medications to build a support system so they can transition off of them when possible. At my clinic, I am not always able to share my personal faith with people to the degree I can in this book, but without Jesus, I would not be where I am today!

HE RESTORES MY SOUL

The difference between medicating a pain and healing what's causing the pain is huge! Don't get me wrong, pain medication can be greatly beneficial at the time of an injury or surgery, but masking the pain is much different than restoring a physical injury or soul to its healthy state. When it comes to the soul, emotional and psychological injuries, if not properly dealt with, can last a life time.

So, we can surrender to God and get the support we need or just keep going. It is key that we take time outs in life when needed to ask God to restore our soul. We can also learn to recognize when we need to take a time out. Anyone who is a basketball fan can tell you when a time out is coming. Whenever the other team goes on a run and makes a couple of big plays and the momentum shifts, all good coaches call a time out. The first thing they do is try to settle their team down or restore their emotions to a good place. Then they talk about needed adjustments to shift the momentum of the game back in their favor. I have learned that when I start drifting into discouragement or fear, I need to take a time out and go to God to let Him adjust my emotions, change the momentum or direction of my life and set me on the right path.

For me, this began with a long time out! The time outs are now shorter and less frequent, but still needed. A championship team knows when to take time outs and re-adjust. If a team does this to win a game, how much more important is it for us to win in life? If we don't, we will just limp through life, hurting ourselves and hurting others.

HURT PEOPLE HURT PEOPLE

This is a common saying and is often very true. This pain creates a cycle that needs to be broken and this requires healing. My father was broken because his father wasn't there when he needed him most. I continued the cycle and even took it to the next level. This would have kept going and probably worsened if either I did not come to God or if I did not personally take responsibility to grow and change to who I am today. I can see in some of my other brothers and sisters how this cycle has continued because they have not yet learned that this cycle can be broken and that a new path can be taken.

BREAKING GENERATIONAL TRENDS AND CURSES

You can see it in the statistics we have already listed, but behind the numbers are real people. Too many times I have sat with people who grew up with abusive alcoholic parents. Then they married people with substance problems, abuse alcohol themselves and then neglect and or abuse each other. Many people who were molested go on to molest others. Even if it doesn't go to this level, many who have been hurt emotionally are so damaged that they have trouble committing or even if they do commit, they struggle to be emotionally connected which unintentionally damages or neglects their partner's needs. These things must be addressed both naturally and spiritually to be overcome or broken off of their lives.

RESTORATION IS POSSIBLE!

Remember that David was thanking God for a restoration that already took place. If you are not familiar with the rest of David's life story, let me share a few key points. David was the last of eight boys, not valued by his father or brothers who often overlooked and belittled him. David was faithful to King Saul who literally tried to hunt him down to kill him. Later, his own men also wanted to kill him after an enemy attacked their city and took all of their belongings, including their wives and children.

In this last situation, after David cried, yes cried, he went to God in prayer. God told him to go after the enemy and that he would regain all of their possessions including their wives and children. This is an example of God restoring physical and financial things in addition to being able to restore our souls. But the reality is that David had to go to God for both strength and direction on how to move forward.

I encourage you today if you are trying to medicate your pain through drugs, alcohol, pornography, sex or even money and achievement, call a time out. Then go to God and ask Him to restore your soul. Trying to self-medicate may mask the pain, but it doesn't fix the problems and usually makes them much worse. When you allow God to restore your soul, your life will be better and those in your life will also greatly benefit from your healing and restoration.

CHAPTER 10

GOD TURNED MY CRISIS INTO OPPORTUNITY

*Insanity is doing the same thing over and over again
and expecting different results.*

- UNKNOWN

Every crisis is an opportunity to grow and learn, to make a change or to stay on the same path. Staying on the same path often results in the same or even greater pain over time. If we want to see a change, we have to be willing to do things differently!

It's funny how stubborn we can be, even when we are inflicting more pain in our own lives. We can inflict pain by our own actions or allowing others to inflict pain on us. Many times, we *allow* others to victimize us verbally, emotionally or even physically and then we blame them. This is a harsh reality, but if we want the pain to stop, we have to own what we allow others to do in our lives.

CRISIS CAN BE THE WAKE-UP CALL TO CHANGE

It's funny how the worst moments in your life can either destroy you or cause you to choose a better path. Several key moments drove me to make change and to continually ask God for help. Having a child at 19 pushed me to responsibility. Having a cocaine seizure ended my drug addiction, and a D.U.I. helped me connect with God in a life changing way. God was with me in the pit of life I had dug, and at the bottom of the pit, He turned my worst moments into springboards for a better future.

FROM BROKENHEARTED TO CEO

I was devastated when my dad passed away. This was a totally unexpected crisis! For decades I wanted my father, then God restored our relationship. I thank God for the years I had with him and the healing that took place between us. Then as we were enjoying a hike in Hawaii, he passed out and died in my arms after I gave him CPR.

This was very shocking and painful to me but also motivational. The brevity of life can be very sobering. Instead of returning to alcohol to medicate my pain, I dug in my heels and committed to moving forward. Up until this point, I had been planning on starting a business, but this experience cemented it. I decided to open the Family Healing Center where I would be the CEO. Some of the best ways we can honor those that have passed is to live well. Part of me wants people to look at me and be happy for my father that I am doing so well.

I also wanted to help men navigate the same type of situations that I faced. Part of my motivation is to give men the help that my father never got. In so many ways, my father was a great man who helped many. It pains me to think what kind of man he could have been had he received help as a young man and over the years. Crisis doesn't let me erase the past, but it can motivate me on how to move forward.

I'm telling you that you can 100% change the direction in your life if you want to. It doesn't matter how many bad choices you have made or how bad your family history is, God can give you a new start.

New starts always begin with a decision and purposeful action. We all want life to be better but few have the courage to make significant changes. Remember how we started the chapter – insanity is doing the same thing over and over again and expecting different results. There have been times when I was following directions on my phone app but a road was closed and the app didn't know so it kept sending me back to the same place. There have been times when I detoured and then started following the directions again and it brought me to the same place that was blocked. This can be difficult when you don't know where you are, but at some point, you have to ignore the directions being given to find a new path around the roadblock. You must have the courage to go in a new direction even when you don't know if it will actually work. I have found that this is the only way to get around the roadblock.

One of the biggest roadblocks in some people's minds is blaming God for their bad circumstances. It's funny because many of these same people aren't thankful to God when things are going right, and don't give Him credit for good things. This can be confusing at times so let's break this down a little.

GOD IS NOT THE AUTHOR OF YOUR PAIN

It's funny how people often blame God for many of life's outcomes. They act like God is in control of what they personally do. On one hand, they don't want God to be responsible or in charge of anything, but instead want to be "free". Then when God gives them the very freedom they want, they get mad at God because of the results from their own choices. I learned that you can't have it both ways. If you want to hold God responsible for the results of your choices, then you have to let Him lead you! I discovered that when I follow God's Word and His leading, I end up in a much better place. Not a perfect place, because life is filled with other people who have their own ideas!

Many also blame God for their circumstances, which are really the result of other people's choices. I was one of those people. But why would God let us make bad decisions?

UNDERSTANDING FREE WILL

God didn't make robots, He made people. God is actually a big believer in freedom. He knows that freedom is needed to truly live. So, what about all those religious people and their rules? Here is the difference. If God gives us rules, they are to prepare us for success. Just like to win a game, rules of that game focus us so that game has order and we know how to play in a way that we can win. Imagine if a basketball player kept throwing the ball into the crowd or if a defender was allowed to tackle someone going up for a dunk. It would be chaos and people would be getting hurt all over the place.

Many times, man makes rules to restrict bad behavior. One of the ways to look at this is rules vs. relationship. When we are in a relationship, rules can be so much different to us. Before I came to the Lord, it was anything goes. A girlfriend who wanted to restrict me from talking to other women – wasn't going to happen! Now that I am married, I purposely don't talk to any woman with romantic or sexual intentions because of the relationship with my wife. What I once thought of as a restrictive rule has now become something that focuses me so that I can have a great relationship with my wife. The only thing that changed was my perspective.

CONFRONTING THE MYTH THAT GOD IS NOT WITH US

After all I did and have been through, I had an epiphany and realized that God was with me the whole time. I no longer ask Him why He wasn't there. I asked Him why He still loved me and was with me even through the worst of times. When everything was falling apart, it was God holding me together. When I was angry at Him, thinking He was not with me, He was carrying me through times I could not walk through myself, and even teaching and healing me along the way.

Many people say things like "God has never done anything for me," but that is simply not true. God is very merciful and protective even when we are in full rebellion to His leadership in our lives. I believe that in eternity, we will find out all of the things that God did for us even when we didn't know it. That car accident that didn't happen. The bullet that missed us. The bad relationship that was avoided when that person didn't like us. God's hand in our lives.

Each day, God gives us breath and a new day to make choices, to grow and change. It is simply a choice of whether or not we will ask Him for His help or just try to be in control of everything ourselves. If you have children, you've probably had the experience of trying to show them the right way to do things but them refusing to listen and then doing things the wrong way. This is part of growing up and can be frustrating, as a parent, but we do the same thing to God. He is telling us the best way, but we often choose our own path.

THE CRISIS IS THE CROSSROAD IN LIFE

In life, there will be times when we must choose what direction we will go. Will we go left, right, straight or turn around? We can allow crisis to be the moment that momentum can shift in our lives. For generations, the men in my family's life were just headed in the wrong direction. I learned to take the crisis or worst moments in my life and find motivation to change the direction of not only my life, but my son's also. I decided that first I would allow God to change my life and I would choose to follow His path. Now, I am helping my son do the same, and I am looking forward to helping my grandchildren in the days ahead to continue on the right path. Maybe you are in a crisis right now. Perfect opportunity to personally change and then change the path you are on. These changes may be big or small, but they are there for the choosing.

HELP FROM GOD AND HELP FROM PEOPLE

Many times, we do not change because we don't have the strength or wisdom needed. I have learned, to truly change, it takes everything I have plus help from God and people. Some may see this as weakness, but I just see it as reality. God made us for relationship, and we need people. For me, I needed friends, pastors, my 12-step sponsor, my church and many others along the way. There is strength in a village, and God did not create us to walk this path alone. Even today, I lean on my wife, friends, and many others to help me continue to grow and change over time.

I have also learned that after different crisis, this support system is needed to continue in the right direction. Over the history of man, the family and community has been the key support system, but with the modern breakdown of many families and communities, we often have to extend our relationships and support beyond our direct family. I've had to learn that this is not a sign of weakness but a sign of wisdom. Maybe you are in a crisis right now or still suffering from the last one. Either way, you are at a crossroad. What is your choice? Will you let your pain drive you to God or away from God? Will you let the crisis drive you to change or will you just keep going? Remember, crisis is an opportunity for change, unless you choose to keep doing the same thing over and over and getting the same results. It sounds crazy but so many people continue to choose crazy...

CHAPTER 11

PLAYING THROUGH THE PAIN

That which does not kill us makes us stronger.[17]

- FRIEDRICH NIETZSCHE

While this quote can be inspirational and even true at times, psychological research tells us that traumatic and difficult experiences actually damage us. On top of that, we often don't acknowledge how damaging our broken relationships and other failures are. We often pride ourselves on how strong we are when we are really being damaged and diminished over time. But as a man, society doesn't let us admit we are hurting. In fact, we are actually encouraged to do things that undermine our long-term health and happiness.

We often then establish a cycle of pain and damage, especially if we never take the time to address them and allow growth and healing to take place. Life often doesn't give us the space for these things unless we take it. But I did not figure this out on my own and there sure wasn't anyone around me who would even think about emotional health. For many years, I did what most people do. No matter what happened, I just kept going. That's what life and people often tell us to do. We then adopt mindsets like this quote that can actually be detrimental to us but don't know what else to do. On the outside I was a strong warrior, but on the inside, I was a broken boy who kept incurring more damage.

Things like sports reinforced this "never quit" mindset. Athletes have to play through pain if they want to win championships. I figured life was the same way; to be successful, I would need to play through the pain of life. As the famous saying goes, "The show must go on." I then found myself "playing injured" because I had bills to pay, a life to live, and needs to be loved but we often live in ways that make the injuries worse. Even when we start making better decisions, we still have to walk forward in pain. We limp forward because that's what men do, it's how we are wired. At some point, injured athletes can be forced to rest and heal. In life, we have to know when it's time to stop limping forward, especially when it's only causing greater injury.

ADMITTING I WAS IN OVER MY HEAD

What this saying means is a picture of a person that does not know how to swim, but they find themselves in water that is deeper than they can stand. In essence, it is the realization that they are about to drown because they have moved from a place of shallow water where they can stand to a place of deeper water. One of the turning points in my life was when I had to humble myself and admit that I didn't have the right plan or all of life's solutions. This caused me to do two things. First, I had to ask God for help, then I had to have the courage to make real changes.

ASK GOD FOR HELP

When I finally got to the end of myself, I realized that I needed God's help – for real. I am not talking about some vague belief in God or a couple of religious habits, but I came to a place of surrendering my life to God and asked for His help. Humility actually invites God and His Power into our lives. Let's look to God's Word about the difference between being arrogant and proud versus being humble.

"God resists the proud, but gives grace to the humble."
-1 PETER 5:5B NKJV

At some point, I realized that I needed God's help in a big way! This required me to be humble, but let's just say I missed "humble" class and no one even mentioned the word to me in a way that would have a positive impact. The only "humbling" I ever wanted to see in my life was when I humbled people with my superiority! For me, I had to come to the end of myself before I was willing to recognize God's superiority.

Looking back, it's kind of funny that it took me so long to admit that God was God. He is the Creator and Ruler of the universe, yet I had trouble humbling myself before Him. This was hard for me because every message I had ever received about being a man demanded that I was strong and in control, and I had to admit that my life was out of control and that I did not have the strength to fix it.

Grace is often defined as "unmerited favor," which means that God helps us even when we don't deserve the level of help He gives us. Another definition is "God's empowerment to do what He has created us to do and be what He created us to be." I had to realize that though I had gifts and talents and had succeeded in many ways, that I was not living out my best purpose in life. I knew there was more and despite my best efforts, I was not able to get there by myself. I needed to ask God to help me and also have the courage to make whatever change He led me to.

The opposite of humility is arrogance and my learned and purposeful arrogance allowed me to succeed in many ways but put me on a path without God and at some point, I was fighting against God and His will for my life.

HAVE THE COURAGE TO MAKE REAL CHANGE

Losing can have a positive impact if it drives us to change and I was running up a list of losses. Usually, before a team wins a championship or a fighter wins a title, they are dealt a painful loss. How they handle the loss makes all the difference. For instance, many boxers progress because of their talent and hard work, but eventually suffer a painful loss because they have either not trained properly or may have the wrong trainer. Yes, they have the talent but their current process or team is insufficient. This painful reality will often cause them to make needed changes. For instance, a boxer may have sufficient conditioning for three or five round fights, but when they are in a 12-round fight, they realize their training is insufficient. Other times, their skill and talent allow them to outpoint and knock out lower level guys, but they run into a brick wall when they hit tougher opponents.

Many will increase training or even switch camps in order to become a champion. They may also hire different coaches, a nutritionist or conditioning coach. Others will maintain their current program and team and end up being a journeyman fighter at best. It's not that they didn't have the talent, they just lacked the courage to make the needed changes. The ones with the courage to change go on to win a world title.

I NEEDED TO CHANGE CAMPS

I was running my own camp because I thought I knew best. The reality was also that even though I was sailing a sinking ship, I was still doing better than just about anyone else I knew. But I learned like the man who represents himself as his own lawyer in a court case, that is usually not a wise decision. I was representing myself and had a religious camp but was totally committed to being the master of my own destiny. The day came when I fired myself and made Jesus my head coach. He changed my daily habits and overall lifestyle so that I could win in life in ways that I never could without Him. But just like the fighter listening to his new coach, I had to learn to follow the leadership of Jesus in my life.

MOVING FROM RELIGION TO RELATIONSHIP

The easiest way to differentiate between religion and relationship is that religion is often a set of rules that try to change or control our behavior from the outside in. A relationship with God transforms us from the inside out. You cannot underestimate the difference between the two! Rules and other outside pressure only create short-term influence. When God changes us from the inside out, it creates a permanent and significant change.

I had been religious my whole life but then made the move and surrendered my life to Jesus as both my Lord and Savior. For years, I had come to God to be my Savior in the sense of saving me from difficult and hard times. Yes, God will help us, at times, when we come to Him, but this is limited when we choose to follow our own path. God bailed me out many times, but I kept going the way I wanted. When I surrendered to Jesus to be my Lord, it made all the difference.

Having Jesus as Lord means that I committed to following His leadership in my life. This meant that even if I didn't understand the direction He was telling me to go, I would still go with it.

LEARNING HOW TO SERVE

Let's just say that servanthood was not at the top of my list. Servanthood requires humility and humility is often the doorway for God to move in our lives. If I truly wanted to walk in God's purpose for my life, I needed to be humble. One of my first mentors told me I was going to serve, and it made no sense to me. I wanted to achieve, not spend my energy doing things to benefit other people. But I had to learn that when I served others, God would make things happen on my behalf. By serving others, it also put me in the presence of people I had to learn from. God showed me that His will happens faster in my life when I walk in humility, serve Him and serve others. I learned by experience that God had my back and best interest, at all times, even when I didn't understand everything going on.

FOLLOWING GOD DOES NOT GUARANTEE A PAIN FREE LIFE BUT A BETTER DESTINATION

Over time, I realized that God would always lead me to a better place. It didn't mean that life would be pain free, but I learned that even though I still had to walk through pain, I could have the confidence that the pain would be less, the journey would be shorter and most importantly, I would continually move in the direction of my life's purpose.

So, I encourage you to ask yourself some tough questions. Are you playing God in your own life or are you letting God be God? I am not simply asking you if you "believe in God" but have you surrendered your life to the leadership of Jesus? Are you willing to make significant changes? Remember our definition of insanity – doing the same thing over and over again and expecting a different result. I don't know if I have ever met anyone that actually likes change. There is a saying that "people don't change until the pain of staying the same is greater than the pain of change". You don't have to get to this point to change but many do. Wisdom says that pain is an indicator that something is wrong. I pray that in the days ahead you will have the courage to change and not just keep walking in unnecessary pain.

SECTION 3

Becoming a Man for Real

CHAPTER 12

REJECTING FALSE MANHOOD

As we struggle forward, we often settle for Band-Aids and temporary solutions. We do the best we can, or most often, what we think is best. We prop up our fragile egos with things that impress others or that satisfy our flesh to help us get through the day. We build sandcastles that look great but are gone when the waves and storms of life hit them. I built my life this way because it was all I knew. We often compare ourselves to others and if we can find a few people we are doing better than, we tell ourselves we are doing well. For years, others envied me as I tried to convince myself that I was good and valuable. It was a show, with little substance. We spend our lives trying to impress others and trying to feed our egos by other people's praise and building up our own pride.

A LESSON FROM *WHITE MEN CAN'T JUMP*

If you are familiar with the old movie, you may know where I am going. This movie was about basketball and featured Woody Harrelson and Wesley Snipes. The movie went back and forth with the two of them being enemies, then friends or what we now call frenemies! The competition began with the white guy hustling the black guy and then the black guy always challenging the white guy to dunk the basketball because no matter how much he tried, the white guy couldn't jump high enough to dunk. Funny movie that has stood the test of time.

But at key moments, the white guy would beat the black guy, which wasn't supposed to happen in the movie and at some point, Woody Harrelson's character told him, *"You rather look good and lose than look bad and win."* [18] This was a picture of my own life. I was looking really good but losing big time in so many ways. Looking good but losing is false manhood and man did I embrace false manhood. Tall, dark and handsome on the outside and confused, selfish and broken on the inside.

I NEEDED TO REDEFINE "MANHOOD"

You can only hit a target if there is a target! I'm not trying to be funny but just sharing the reality that my friends and I had no real definition of manhood outside of who could get the most girls, money in our pocket and driving a nice car. Nothing wrong with having a beautiful woman, some cash and a nice car, but I found out that there was a whole lot more to manhood than this. In fact, I had to change my dictionary.

EXCHANGING MY URBAN DICTIONARY FOR GOD'S DEFINITIONS

I had let my hormones and friends define manhood for me, but I had to trade the voices I was listening to. Here are a couple of things that I learned from the Bible and true men of God. First, God calls men to be faithful to their wives. This may sound strange to some, but for the first 34 years of my life, I literally never met a man who had been faithful to their girlfriend or even their wife. There is power in commitment. Commitment brings stability and causes growth to happen. When a man bounces from woman to woman, he never has to grow up. When a man is in a long-term relationship with a woman, he has to deal with real issues and deal with himself.

Dating different women and not keeping commitments allows a man to be immature because by the time someone calls him on his behavior, he's gone on to the next victim until that falls apart, too. I don't think that I could tell you what love was until I was close to 40 years old.

THE DIFFERENCE BETWEEN LUST AND LOVE

What many people call love is really an extremely inferior feeling called lust. Lust is a passionate desire for something that really doesn't belong to us. It is driven by hormones and fleshly desires that are physical and can even be animal like. There is no depth or quality to lust. It's kind of like an uncontrollable fire that is intense, can be exciting, but in the end it is just destructive. Our society is filled with lust, but true love is rare and even unimaginable for some. Lust takes, love gives. Lust cheapens, love makes things more valuable. At the end of the day, lust is desiring something that can't last. Like a child building a sandcastle by the sea shore, it is fun to build but simply gets washed away often within a few minutes of being built.

LOVE PROTECTS AND PROVIDES

True love is much different because it protects and provides for a woman and children. Real love is sacrificial and puts others ahead of self. This was revolutionary to me because all I had ever known was lust as a feeling that came and went, and when the feeling went, so did I. Also, the idea of protecting a woman's emotions was new to me. I had always thought of women to be enjoyed, not loved and honored. God had to change the way I thought.

LETTING GOD RENEW MY MIND

I had always wanted God to help me. But then, I came to a place where I knew I needed God to help me. Something happened that I had never expected. One of the main ways God helped me was to change the way I thought. I don't mean that He just gave me new knowledge, but that He literally changed that way I thought. The following verse describes what literally happened in my life. My thinking changed from how the world had shaped my mind to God literally reshaping the way I thought and the way my mind worked.

Do not conform to the pattern of this world but be transformed by the renewing of your mind. Then you will be able to test and approve what God's will is—his good, pleasing and perfect will.
-ROMANS 12:2

When I truly committed my life to following Jesus, I began to see and understand God's Word in a totally different way. This verse painted a picture of my past life and then what I experienced as I studied God's Word, and my faith grew. The Apostle Paul was writing to the Romans who were famous for their parties, games in the Coliseum, watching animals kill each other and even feeding humans to the lions, as well as having wild sex lives. They had been conditioned to not only think these things were normal, but to passionately chase after these things. Their minds had been "conformed" to follow a pattern of having no morality or value of human life. This was not only normal to them, but to be celebrated. History tells us that this breakdown had a big contribution to the fall of the Roman Empire which was the most powerful empire in the world for several centuries. I had also seen that my life was being destroyed by my past mindset, but God was speaking to me through the writing of the Apostle Paul to allow

God to "renew my mind" or cause me to think differently.

TRANSFORMATION IS A PROCESS

"Renewing of the mind" is much bigger than gaining new information or increasing a knowledge base. This is a part of the transformation process that God wants to take place, but we will not experience a true powerful transformation if our goal is to simply learn or experience new information.

We are taught to think one way by the world, but God wants to teach us to think and act in a different way. This is both a spiritual and intellectual process. Yes, new information must be learned but if we are to understand and desire to do God's will, then we must engage in a spiritual process. Many people never have the opportunity to have their mind transformed because they are too angry at God to benefit from His help.

This transformation goes way beyond going to church. I had to read the Bible daily, listen to solid teaching and have discussions with other men to figure out how to apply God's Word in my life on a daily basis. Too many men go to church but don't consistently and passionately pursue God each day. If you want God to really change your life, true and lasting growth happens a little bit each day but adds up over time.

ANGRY AT GOD?

Over the years, I have met many people who are angry at God for what has happened in their lives. This is understandable because people often feel that God is responsible for everything that happens, but thinking God is deliberately hurting people is simply not true. Think about it. Do you think that God is sitting around causing car accidents, purposely starving children and making people hate and kill each other? If that was true, then yes, it would make sense for people to be mad at God.

The question is what is God's will? This verse starts off by saying to not "conform to the pattern of the world", which means the trends, behaviors, values and customs that people follow. After our minds are transformed, "Then you will be able to test and approve what God's will is." This makes it clear that certain things are God's will and certain things are not. On top of that, people don't automatically know if something is God's will so people can choose actions and lifestyles that are not according to His purpose which sends them in the wrong direction. God's will is found in God's Word – the Bible. Things that are outside of God's will are called "sin."

UNDERSTANDING WHO GOD IS

The easiest way to define sin is something that is outside of God's will. To know what God's will is, we can look to the Bible. Some of God's characteristics include:

God is love
Whoever does not love does not know God, because God is love.
-1 JOHN 4:8
God is righteous
The Lord is righteous in all his way and faithful in all he does.
-PSALM 145:17
God is faithful
Let us hold unswervingly to the hope we profess, for he who promised is faithful. -HEBREWS 10:23
God is fair and just
He is the Rock, his works are perfect, and all his ways are just.
A faithful God who does no wrong, upright and just is he.
-DEUTERONOMY 32:4

So, if you consider these few verses that describe God, He is loving, righteous, faithful and just. This means anything that goes against these principles is not God's will. Remember, God created us for relationship and in order to have genuine relationship, you have to give people the opportunity to either reject or accept that relationship. So, when God gives people free will, they have the freedom to not only choose if they want to have a relationship with God, but they can also either accept or reject His Ways.

The word "sin" comes from a word that means missing the target. So, when people "sin" they are doing something outside of God's will. This is why, in the Ten Commandments, God tells us not to do things like lie, steal, kill, cheat on our spouse etc., because these things end up hurting people, and that is outside of God's will and character. Before I chose to truly follow Jesus, I constantly made choices that rejected God's will and embraced false manhood. All the factors I was using to measure manhood had more to do with fleshly sinful desires than being a man who protects and provides for the people in his life.

PROTECT AND PROVIDE

True love does two things – it protects and it provides. Protection means taking care of someone's emotions and providing an atmosphere for them to grow and prosper. Let me finish with one clarification about "providing" for someone. When I was dating women, one of the things I always ran from were gold diggers, women who were only after money and gifts. It's simple, men get sex, the gold diggers get material things. This is not what I mean by providing for someone. In fact, in marriage provision is reciprocal. Husbands and wives provide emotional support and encouragement, along with the physical benefits of a healthy sexual life and many other things. Parents provide the emotional support, stability and atmosphere for children to grow and develop in a safe and wholesome atmosphere.

One thing I have learned is that it is never too late to grow. I had many false beliefs, was aiming at the wrong targets and did not have a good road map to follow. I learned that each day, I could either challenge myself to be something greater or just accept what the world wanted to hand me. I learned that God's ways are the best. I simply had to reject false manhood to be able to embrace true manhood: God's plan all along.

CHAPTER 13

AGE 26

When I was a child, I talked like a child, I thought like a child,
I reasoned like a child. When I became a man,
I put the ways of childhood behind me.
-1 CORINTHIANS 13:11

Around age 26, something happened: I started to grasp manhood. It was like the channel changed and I saw life differently. Maybe the light bulb went on. This may happen at different times for different people. For some it is earlier, for others it may not happen until even later in life. For my father, I'm not sure it ever happened. At 26, I sure didn't have the answers, but I realized that I needed to change the game I was playing. I might have been going in style, but I was on the road to nowhere.

BRAIN MATURITY IMPACTS BEHAVIOR

Renewing the mind and spiritual growth are absolute priorities. But, there is also the reality of physical development which can greatly impact the quality of our lives long term. Modern science is now telling us that full brain development doesn't occur until sometime in the mid-twenties or even up into the early thirties.[19]

My experience was a physical change. Something happened to me that dealt with physical growth and maturity. One of the mistakes people make is that they do not take a holistic view of life. I am a person of faith, but the mistake that some faith people make is they over spiritualize things. They think that everything is caused by God or the devil. Let me help you, if you show up to work late too many times, it wasn't the devil's scheme that got you fired; it was a lack of self-discipline.

The mistake that secular people make is they do not consider spiritual things legitimate in a "scientific sense". Most people don't realize that most of the men who established different scientific disciplines were Christian men who believed in the Bible. In fact, some saw the responsibility of science to explain and define God's creation. From a professional view, we can look at the physical and the spiritual as different disciplines. They don't cancel each other out; at times, they complement each other, and at other times, they are just different. For instance, if you ask a zoologist, botanist and geologist to explain a region, you will get three different views. One will focus on the animal population, one on the plant life and the third on the land structure. They can complement each other, but you can't use each one to understand or fully explain the other. But for me, at 26, I entered a different physical and cognitive place. I still lacked many things, but the light bulb got a little brighter.

DAD IS OFTEN MISSING AT THE MOST CRUCIAL TIME

If science is telling us that a young man's brain is not fully developed, and they may not be thinking clearly and maturely until at least their mid-twenties, this demonstrates an even greater need for a father in these times. Parental discipline is designed to guide, and even control children at times. Especially for boys, the strength of a man giving direction or even being an obstacle to bad decisions and self-destructive behaviors is needed. Recently, a woman told me that raising boys and girls is different. Specifically, she said that part of raising boys is just to keep them alive! The testosterone and physicality of boys makes them active and adventurous, and a father's role is to help them spend that energy constructively, and yes, keep them from harming themselves at times.

And taking nothing away from mothers, a man's voice and physical presence carries weight in a young man's world. This does not mean that men are better than women, just different. As different foods provide different nutrients to make the body healthy, men simply provide different and essential things that young men need.

LET'S GO BACK TO LOVE – PROTECTING AND PROVIDING

The role of a father's love during childhood, adolescence, teen and young adult years protects and provides. Like an umbrella in the rain, it is a father's job to protect their child from anything or anyone that would lead them in the wrong direction or harm them in any way. Take away the umbrella in the rain storm and a person will get soaked. Not only was the protection absent in my friend's lives, as well as my own, but we purposely ran toward and into every destructive thing we could get to.

As for protection, no chance, and as for provision, most of us benefitted from having great mothers. Manhood provision was somewhere between lacking and non-existent. Now you have a group of young men who, for the most part, were on their own. We were like a group of five-year old's in a newly painted room, given unlimited cookies and juice and then given crayons, before being told not to write on the walls for the next 5 hours. Needless to say, even when we were given good instructions, we did not follow.

HOW ABOUT GUIDANCE AND WISDOM?

A father's role is to give daily and ongoing strategic guidance and wisdom for all of the choices and decisions that a young man faces. This was non-existent as my father wasn't there and I was in rebellion to my step-father. I was like a sailor who didn't know how to steer a ship amongst waves and without a compass to know where to turn.

But at 26, there was a noticeable shift that took place. In a sense, I realized that life was real and that at some point, I had to get my act together, grow up and get going in the right direction. Like many men in my situation, I realized that change was needed but didn't know where to start. I thank God that something physical did kick in because that was all I really knew. I was spiritually disconnected from God, and things like emotional maturity and health were not yet on my radar.

MAKING A CONSCIOUS DECISION TO #GROWTHEHECKUP

There is a hashtag that is often used to confront immature behavior in a funny way on social media, #growtheheckup. Not sure where it came from, but it communicates a simple reality that we all need to make a conscious decision to grow up. For me, this was age 26. Looking back, I did not instantly mature at 26, but I did begin a process and direction change in my life.

It was painful to look in the mirror and not like what I saw. In fact, one time when I looked in the mirror, I actually saw a horrible creature like thing looking back at me. I think God allowed me to see what I looked like on the inside. When I saw this, I was shook.

I was shook mostly because I realized that the ugly thing that I saw was real and it was me. I also realized that even if I could blame others for many things, I was ultimately responsible for myself.

GOD, WHAT DO I DO WITH THIS?

One of the keys is to not get paralyzed when you are in a bad place. My friend and co-author learned to pray, "God, what do I do with this?" when dealing with difficult and unfair situations. Too many people become paralyzed as they play the blame game. I could blame my dad, my mom for certain things, my step-father, my friends, God and on and on, but none of that changes anything, and I still have to deal with me! We also can get stuck when we dwell on the "why" questions of why people did this or that or "why did God let this happen?" etc., but they don't get us anywhere. So instead of playing the blame game, you can turn your problem into a prayer, "God, what do I do with this?" I've learned that when I look to God for direction, He gives it to me.

GOD GIVES WISDOM WITHOUT BEATING US UP

So many times, people confuse what people do with who God is. My experience with church was both good and bad. I grew up with a sense of community, with people who spoke about values that were good and true, but many times, their actions contradicted their teachings. First, they often didn't live up to the moral standards that were talked about. Secondly, some of these same people then turned around and were overly judgmental to me and others. That is a big turn off. For me and many others, it can make us shy away from asking for help from these people because we know we will be judged and pay a price for asking for help! Worst of all, we often transfer our feelings and hold them against God, preventing us from going to Him for the help we need.

But God's Word teaches us that God is not like some of the people we know who are fake and phony. One of the greatest things we need is wisdom and God is the greatest source.

If any of you lacks wisdom, you should ask God, who gives
generously to all without finding fault, and it will be given to you.
-JAMES 1:5

This verse points us to God when we need wisdom. The writer, James, says we should ask God to give us wisdom. He then paints the picture that God gives wisdom generously. Sometimes, we have been so conditioned by people who are selfish and self-seeking that we have learned to not ask people for anything. In addition to this, men often have pride, making them feel the need to be strong and do things on their own, but God's Word is instructing us differently.

My favorite part of this verse is that God gives us a generous amount of wisdom "without finding fault!" God knows that we need wisdom and that many times we make bad decisions and get into bad situations because we lacked wisdom. I know for me, I have paid the price with people when I have admitted that I made wrong decisions or that I did not know any better. Too many times, people think that this gives them the right to beat you up. This is another reason that we should look to God, our heavenly Father, as our source.

SO, WHAT YOU GONNA DO?

Maybe you are like I was at 26, and the light bulb has kicked on, or maybe you haven't experienced enough pain yet. But if you do want your life to go in a different direction, I think it begins with a long hard look in the mirror. Just be real and honest with yourself. I do caution you though not to get stuck. Where are you now and where do you want to be? From an intellectual and emotional point of view, you may have to #growtheheckup! From a spiritual point of view, you may need to stop running from God and ask Him for wisdom.

If you have had a bad experience with religion or religious people, don't let that hinder you or be an excuse for not walking with God. God is better than people, period. And there are a lot of really good religious people, in fact, I consider myself one of them.

For me, it was at age 26. You may be older or younger, but the same principles apply. Physical maturity will take place, and we don't have control over that. What we do have control over is our spiritual and emotional maturity. I suffered neglect and lack of development in both of these areas. Maybe you have paid the same price as me. My advice is simple: ask God to start filling in the gaps, make the right choices yourself, and surround yourself with people who will help you become everything God created you to be. Some growth is determined by our efforts, but other growth comes from God when we walk with Him. Either way, we have to walk it out over time.

CHAPTER 14

THE LITTLE BOY INSIDE ME WAS CRYING TO BE A MAN

One of the challenges of growing up without a father is not having or knowing who to talk to. Deep down inside, I sensed my own greatness, but so many times, it felt like a tidal wave of doubt was sweeping me away and when I reached out for help, there was no hand for me to grab. I just wanted to hear someone tell me that I could do it and that I would be ok. I cried out for words of encouragement and all I heard was silence.

DEEP THOUGHTS

Deep thoughts, they run through my mind
Some all at the same time.
Will I be this great man or just someone scattered in a world
full of chatter?
Will I WIN, or WILL I LOSE?

NO! I tell myself just keep Fighting to WIN.
Because I am my # 1 FAN

When will these thoughts stop, because they're so very frightening?

I am determined to be the best,
So, I keep putting myself through some serious tests.

But, then I questioned what's to measure my best?
I have nothing to compare to.
Is there anyone out there who has a clue, to show me what to do?

I need somebody to believe in me
OH! GOD says He does,
So, I challenge Him every day.

I BEG him to Show me a MIRACLE
OH, I'm Breathing, that's a miracle in itself.
So, I just Pray and ASK GOD to help me through this day
and to SHOW me a way, so I will not go ASTRAY.........

On the outside, I was a 6 foot 3, 220-pound man, but on the inside, there was a little boy crying. So many men are strong and impressive on the outside but broken and hurting on the inside. Physical growth happens automatically when we eat and sleep over time, but emotional, psychological and spiritual growth must be intentional. As an adult, I had to learn to feed these areas that my father never fed when I was growing up, ones he still couldn't care for as an adult. I had to learn to live differently if that little boy on the inside was to ever grow up to match the man on the outside.

THE STATISTICS ARE UGLY AND PAINFUL

Many times, we look at the statistics, particularly of fatherless boys and often within the African-American population. The effects are clearly documented. My goal here is not to discuss the reasons for all this but to talk about solutions and how to move forward. These dynamics occur in all racial and socio-economic groups but are highest in African-American populations, particularly in the poor communities and inner city. One of my mentors, Bill Powell, has been a strong encourager, especially when pushing to complete and release this book. Decades of practical experience and the statistical data shows that 70-80% of problems in African-American men coming to counseling can be traced to a lack of fathering as a child.

I see the same thing at the Family Healing Center where I serve as owner and CEO. Part of the problem is that these issues developed literally over centuries from slavery, to segregation, to the breakdown of the family, that created generations of families surviving on welfare which actually encouraged having more children out of wedlock. This is reality. Another reality is the stigma in the African-American population and even more so when it comes to men receiving counseling and mental health care. My prayer is that we can break this stigma and provide people the encouragement and help they need to break these cycles. The Family Healing Center also serves men and women from every ethnic and socio-economic background because the issues we are discussing in this book affect people from every background.

DEPRESSION, LOW SELF-ESTEEM AND SELF-HATRED

These can be caused by many things but one of the most common is a lack of security, hope and positive input. Depression is often the result of not being able to see a better future. Low self-esteem often results from a lack of positive encouragement coupled with excessive criticism. Self-hatred is when a person not only lacks a sense of self-worth but also begins to dislike and even hate self. A father's job is to speak life into their children, to recognize and encourage their gifts and strengths, and overall, to speak forth a child's value and worth. God's Word says, "the power of the tongue is life and death" (Proverbs 18:21). So, words either bring forth life or death in a person. I think this is most powerful in the emotional realm. Negative words kill hope and self-esteem. A lack of positive words leads to a lack of life, hope, joy and happiness in a person.

EMOTIONAL MALNUTRITION

We all learn in school that malnutrition will hurt us physically, but who talks about emotional malnutrition? Just like a lack of physical nutrients can physically stunt growth, a lack of emotional input can stunt emotional growth and well-being. A lack of calcium will lead to weak bones. Insufficient protein or calories can stunt physical height, muscular development, and myriads of diseases can be traced back to an insufficient vitamins or minerals. Lack of affirmation from a father can cause all kinds of emotional deficiencies which later translate into unhealthy decisions and lifestyles.

I HAD TO LEARN TO FEED THE LITTLE BOY INSIDE

Big man on the outside and broken little boy on the inside. This is not only me but literally hundreds of men that I have talked to. Reality can be a tough thing to handle. Nobody chooses the cards they are dealt in life, but we all have a choice regarding how we play the hand. I needed to learn to throw out the bad cards and get some new ones! I had to recognize where I was deficient and feed those areas. I needed strong men to teach me to be a man. I connected with these men in my church. They spoke life into me and didn't let me settle for being less than who God created me to be. They loved me and pushed me to be better. They taught me to be humble and serve men that were further along than me, and in the process, gain from their knowledge, love and experience.

I HAD TO LEARN TO LOVE MYSELF

When a child does not receive the love of their father, they often question if they are loveable at all. If the very one who is supposed to model love to me can't even acknowledge my existence, maybe I'm not worthy of being acknowledged? This may sound strange to some, but it is easy to see how a child feels this way. The problem is that if we don't acknowledge, confront and overcome this mindset, we will continue to take this thought process with us for the rest of our lives!

Because I didn't love myself, I couldn't really receive the love of others. I had many women who were good women and truly loved me, but I was not able to receive it. I was like a starving man who refused to eat the very food he so desperately needed. So, in the area of receiving love, I was malnourished. Let me explain.

I HAD TO LEARN TO RECEIVE LOVE

In God's plan, a little boy should receive love from several sources. The most important source of love is God Himself, followed by the love of father and mother, then family, followed by friends. This begins to paint a picture of my emotional malnourishment that had me living as a man in the physical sense, but a broken boy emotionally. First, I did not know how much God loved me or how to receive His love. My father did not yet know God for himself, so he was absent and did not teach me about God's love nor was he able to love me himself. My mother loved me very much but was married to a step-father who did not have a pure love for me. At times, I think that hindered me receiving my mother's love in certain ways, and my interactions with him and his verbal and physical abuse made matters worse. Then my church experience was more religious than relational. It was more about acting right and avoiding sin and bad decisions, than knowing and understanding who God really was. My extended family also shared some love, but it was not what it could have been because they were not really serving God and walking in His love. As far as my friends, there was loyalty and friendship but not the kind of soul satisfying love I needed. When it came to girlfriends, many had strong emotions and what they would call love, but I was not looking for genuine life-giving love.

I SUFFERED FROM EMOTIONAL MALNUTRITION

I was either receiving no love or a diminished form of love from the main sources of love that I should have received. Just like a malnourished child doesn't choose to be malnourished or have stunted growth, neither did I choose to be emotionally stunted in my growth. No one chooses to be stuck in an underdeveloped emotional state, but just like there are natural consequences of a lack of physical nutrition, there are consequences from emotional malnutrition. Just as it is a parent's job to supply physical nutrients, it is also a parent's job to supply emotional nutrients for a child to grow in emotional maturity.

THE LOVE OF A GIRLFRIEND IS DIFFERENT THAN THE LOVE OF A WIFE

You have to look to God's Word to understand this. God created marriage to be a lifelong commitment between one man and one woman. This relationship is meant to provide lifelong stability for husband and wife and for children. Culturally, this is the norm around the world. Yes, there are exceptions, but if you look at the entire world across all cultures and all times, man has seen the benefit of lifelong commitment no matter what background they come from.

Modern dating changes all of the dynamics. Sex without commitment and relationships driven by sex instead of commitment. This does a couple of things. First, it is more passion and lust driven than based on true love. It also creates a falsehood, especially for men, that there are many options instead of the value of making a strong commitment to one woman. This creates a different dynamic where the goal is feelings and passion that are not be based on anything with long term benefits. This also puts woman at a disadvantage and puts a man in a place where he can take a woman's emotions and passions for granted because there is always another woman out there.

I responded to my girlfriends and even my first wife's love more like a ride on the roller coaster at the amusement park than something of substance. This hurt these women, but also myself, as I did not grow from their love. So many women give their love away to a man who either isn't interested or even if he sincerely wants to be loved, doesn't know how to receive it. I was guilty of this many times.

WOMEN PAY A PRICE FOR THEIR MEN'S LACK OF EMOTIONAL GROWTH

So many wonderful women are playing the wrong game, expecting to receive a man's lifetime love and commitment from an emotionally broken boy who just lives in a man's body. Broken men come in all shapes and sizes. Some are highly educated and some are high school dropouts. Some run businesses and are rich while others collect welfare and unemployment. Some are politicians or movie stars while others are janitors in the buildings where these powerful men work.

I work with wealthy men who had parents who were married for decades, but their father or both their parents were so consumed with making money and gaining power that they never really loved or raised their children. Just look how the rich and famous are always in the news with their divorces. Many times, this is because there is a broken boy inside of that strong powerful business man, politician or movie star. These are basic principles for all mankind and the outer things are just a covering for what's real on the inside.

GROWING UP EMOTIONALLY IS A PROCESS THAT MUST BE ENGAGED

You can't fix something if you don't know it is broken! I had to recognize the gaps and brokenness within me. For years, I was on autopilot and just kept going. Only when the pain was overwhelmingly significant and no longer ignorable, did I come to this realization. Some men will stay on autopilot their entire lives, others have been so hurt that they are paralyzed and simply can't move forward without help. Then there are those who are tired of the road they are on and even tired of the road their family has been on and are ready for change.

Change is painful. Healing is also painful! This may seem like an oxymoron. How can healing be painful? Remember when you got splinters as a kid and someone had to dig it out? It was always painful until they got it out and then came the sigh of relief. What about surgery? The recovery from surgery and rehabilitation is often very painful. The more you are able to push through the pain of change and healing, the faster and further you will come.

At some point, I decided to go after healing and growth with the same or even more passion that I went after partying, sex and making money. If I had passion and energy for those things, how much more should I devote my passion and energy to things that brought health and wholeness to my life.

You can do it. My recommendations are simple. First, walk with God and ask Him to strengthen you each day. Surround yourself with people who are committed to helping you grow and be everything God created you to be. I only found this in my church because people there were there to serve God and help men like me, not just out for themselves. Then build healthy relationships with friends and your wife or future wife. I had to stop living for the moment and think long term and about my eternity. When my thinking changed, the changes were easier to make and stick with.

I am not sure if the boy on the inside has caught up to the man on the outside, but it's definitely a lot closer and I am committed to growing daily for the rest of my life.

CHAPTER 15

ENJOYING FLAWED AND COMPLICATED PEOPLE

One of the greatest challenges in life is trying to enjoy broken people. Truthfully, on some level, we are all flawed and complicated. Some people are just more offensive in their brokenness. Whether it's our parent, our spouse and even our children, I have had to learn to purposely enjoy the good in people even when some of their behaviors are offensive and even self-destructive. Sometimes we spend so much time focusing on the negative within people, that we don't enjoy the positive. I see this in my practice all the time. People are so angry and hurt by what others do, they can't enjoy the good that is within them. This doesn't mean to deny reality but to enjoy what people have to offer as we navigate how to approach them in a way that can help bring positive change.

CONFRONTING PEOPLE IS NEEDED

Part of enjoying my dad required confronting him at times. The reason people don't enjoy people is because they are angry or feel victimized by their behaviors. I had to learn when to confront my dad about his inconsistencies and lies. By confronting him, two things happened. First, I was able to show my dad areas where he still needed to grow and change.

It helped me because I felt better when I released and expressed my negative feelings. The reality is when you confront people like this, you get mixed results. At times, my dad would admit wrong doing and try to work on it, other times, ingrained ways of thinking and bad habits would win the day. Confronting the issue gave me freedom because I was able to not be controlled by disappointment or anger, and then I was able to enjoy the good parts about my dad. This is often not ideal but is reality with people.

THINGS WILL NEVER BE PERFECT

My dad grew up relationally distant from his dad and probably had more gaps than I did. Yes, he changed, and things got better in so many ways, but I realized that things would never be perfect with us. The reality is that in any relationship, usually one person's brokenness collides with the other person's brokenness and that's when conflict and problems occur. We must have wisdom and know when to confront and when to let things go, when to fight for what is right or just accept that people are flawed. One thing I have learned is that when someone has a character flaw, it will come up again so if I don't have the time or this isn't the place, I will have another time to address it!

In marriage, the same principle applies. I see so many couples who are fighting about things and are stuck. They have both done wrong things, but often each emphasize what they personally did right and then magnify what the other person didn't do right. It becomes a vicious cycle where people keep lists of offenses that block the blessings that the other person actually has to offer.

I had to learn to confront people's wrong actions and attitudes, but then let things go. I learned that you can pressure people to make temporary changes, but true long-lasting change comes from God changing people, and them embracing the need to change themselves. If you hold onto the reality of the wrongs that have been done to you, they will eat away at your soul. We often wish and hope for things that may never come. I had to learn when to have hope in certain things and other times, I needed to just deal with harsh realities. I realized that at times, hoping in people for certain things is an act of foolishness that only brings pain and disappointment. Like many things, this is simple in theory but more complicated in real life.

HOPE DEFERRED MAKES THE HEART SICK

God's Word has been one of my greatest educators because it teaches unchanging truth in a world that can be very confusing and unstable. For years, I had hoped to be re-united with my father, for my father to love me, and for my father to be proud of me. For decades, this hope was unmet. Let's look to the book of Proverbs which is also called the book of wisdom to see what God thinks about unmet hope.

Hope deferred makes the heart sick,
but a longing fulfilled is a tree of life. -PROVERBS 13:12

So, my heart was sick because of the dashed hopes I had experienced from my father's absence, but then God did a miracle and brought us together again. My heart began to heal in so many ways as certain longings began to be fulfilled. I got to know my father and we even started a business together. We spent time working and laughing about many things. I began to understand the man "I was just like" and was grateful for the good aspects of this.

I was also grateful that God had gotten a hold of my heart and I could now see how unhealthy and destructive patterns of behavior are transferred from generation to generation. These transfers are both natural and spiritual. Natural through genetics and physical surroundings and spiritual because our choices open the door to either God's or to destructive and even evil forces. That's why walking with God is important in order to open the door to His power and blessings and to shut the door on evil forces. I learned that these forces are absolutely present, and our choices effect what power and authority we let into our lives.

So many of my hopes had gone from being deferred and making my heart sick to being fulfilled and giving me new life. This is the type of power God has to change a person's life. This was challenging as I was getting to know my father for the first time as an adult. At times, my emotions were all over the place. Happy, sad, joyful, angry, you name it, I felt it!

LEANING ON GOD

God had become my source, and because of that, I was better able to enjoy time with my earthly father. Yes, my father was now a source, but God had become THE source in my life! This may not make sense to you if you have not yet learned that this is possible. It was sure new to me! I learned to lean on God as the One who defined me, not my biological father. I learned that God loved me and was leading and encouraging me. God was also the One I looked to for help and fulfillment. These things took the focus off my father and allowed me to enjoy the good things about him, even in the midst of his inconsistencies and behaviors that would have destroyed our relationship if I was looking for him to be my most important source.

SECTION 4

New Life and a Bright Future

CHAPTER 16

HEALING IS A PROCESS

If time heals all wounds, then why are there so many
ticked off old people walking around.[20]

GARRISON WYNN

In both my personal and professional experience as CEO of the Family Healing Center, I have learned that time by itself does not bring healing. Healing is a process and the more deliberate the process, the faster and more complete healing can be. The problem for many people is they don't know they need healing. When I messed up and ended up in jail or got caught cheating and my first wife left me, I would have said I needed to get it together, but if you told me that I needed healing I would have probably laughed and told you I just needed to cover my tracks better.

I often shake my head when I meet people in their 60s and 70s and they are clearly wounded and angry from things that literally happened 50-60 years ago! We live in the world of "I'm ok" or in modern terms "I'm good" when people are hurting and in need of healing. I pray that you will take a minute and ask yourself if you have been broken in some way, causing you to live in fear or to make wrong decisions that you continue to pay for. If you do need healing, please take it seriously. I found when I asked God for help and sought help from my church, as well as professional clinical counseling, I made the best progress.

IS HEALING A PRAYER AWAY?

Maybe, but probably not. Don't get me wrong, I believe in the power of prayer and there have been times when God healed me or set me free in one prayer. I quit cocaine with one prayer, which just happened to be encouraged by a cocaine seizure. But some religious people and even pastors have wrong thinking at times. God can heal you with a prayer, but many times, healing is a process. The Bible actually says there is wisdom in having many counselors. In this context it is more talking about living successfully, but the principle is there. Sometimes people who are not religious are actually easier to help in the counseling field because they see a need to allow emotional healing to be a process where their participation and the input of others is needed.

DEDICATE THE TIME AND ENERGY TO HEAL

Just like a broken leg takes 4-8 weeks to heal, emotional healing is a process that takes time. This is important because some people teach that this type of healing only takes one prayer. Yes, this is possible, and I have experienced instant healing and seen it in others, but I have also experienced and seen that it often takes a process. Some would say this thinking is a lack of faith, which is possible, but a person can have strong faith and still need time and help to overcome many things.

The more broken you are, the longer it may take to heal. Think about it this way, the more malnourished you are, the longer it takes to replenish lost nutrients and rebuild the unhealthy weak structures. I had to acknowledge the gaping holes and gaps inside me; the areas that were not fed. Then I had to purposely allow myself to heal and to receive the nourishment I needed. This meant forming better relationships, habits, and a new lifestyle. I had to walk away from destructive habits, wrong thinking and even people. If I wanted to heal, I had to leave behind the things that broke me. I had to learn to feed my spirit and not just my flesh. With God's help, supportive men and a different lifestyle, the healing process began and is still going on today.

There is a big difference between someone who didn't eat for a couple of days and someone who has been malnourished for several years. In the same way, someone who scraped their knee heals a whole lot quicker than someone who broke both legs in a car accident. Recuperation and healing vary in so many situations. I was literally emotionally malnourished my entire childhood, teen and young adult years due to the absence of my father.

For my wife, she learned about her dad as an adult through reading his obituary. Talk about gaps. So, this is not a male only issue. But the reality is that my wife was less affected from her father being absent than me because of the tremendous relationship she had with her mom who was able to feed into her needs in a greater way from female to female. Other women I know have been devastated either by the absence of or the abuse from their fathers. The statistics also paint a clear picture of females growing up without fathers and the increased problems with lower education achievement, increased out of wedlock pregnancy, etc.

FORGIVENESS CAN BE A LARGE PART OF HEALING

I learned about forgiveness as a Bible concept. Forgiveness sure wasn't a high priority in my world growing up. I'm not talking about the sorry "my bad" type of forgiveness, I am talking about real deal forgiving someone who did you wrong. First, I didn't expect people to forgive me be-cause I chose to do what I did, period. Secondly, I wasn't forgiving anyone who played me; that's for sure.

But, then I began to understand that I needed forgiveness for the wrong things I had done, and that Jesus went to the cross to literally pay the penalty for my sins and was willing to forgive me if I wanted to receive that forgiveness. I asked Jesus to forgive me and that's when He became real in my life. Then, as I read and heard teaching from the Bible, I began to realize that God wanted me to forgive others the same way He for-gave me. This was new to me, but I began to learn that just like I received freedom and grew from God forgiving me, others would gain freedom and the opportunity to grow if I forgave them. However, the biggest thing I learned was that when I forgave others, I became free!

DEFINING FORGIVENESS

Before we get into what forgiveness is, let's talk about what forgive-ness is not. First, forgiveness does not mean what someone did was ok or that they can continue doing hurtful things. Forgiveness is also not rec-onciliation. Reconciliation means a relationship is mended in such a way that the past offenses no longer cause tension; the relationship is strong enough that what has happened in the past doesn't hinder the current state of the relationship.

Reconciliation involves forgiveness, but it also involves sorrow for past actions and repentance or changed behavior by the offender. Forgiveness frequently occurs without the reconciliation of the relationship taking place, especially if the offender has no sorrow for hurting a person and hasn't truly embraced their own personal growth and change. Forgive-ness should never allow abuse to continue. We don't have the power to stop abandonment or neglect, but everyone has the power to stop abuse.

There is also a strong possibility that many people who have been abused will need help to get out of that relationship, as well as support afterwards to grow strong again. There is no shame in this. In fact, if you have been abused I would say its mandatory that you get help. If you have been abused, PLEASE reach out for help.

I like the definition that my friend and co-author, Jack Redmond, gives to forgiveness: *"Forgiveness is letting go of other people's brokenness."*

In essence, you are taking the lead in the situation and not the person who has caused the damage. You see, you may not be able to help other people change and in reality, some people do horrible things and don't care. Many times, people are holding on to what people have done to them and the other person couldn't care less; they are on to abusing or neglecting someone else! Forgiveness says that I am letting go of what you did to me so that it no longer hurts me. It is refusing to carry someone else's brokenness and refusing to allow their brokenness to define you.

TRUE FORGIVENESS IS A GOD THING

For me, learning to forgive had to be learned by receiving forgiveness for all that I had done. When I truly realized that God had forgiven ALL that I had done, the way I viewed forgiveness changed. Many people don't actually understand how much they are hurting people. Listen to what Jesus said as He literally hung on the cross:

Jesus said, "Father, forgive them, for they do not know what they are doing." And they divided up his clothes by casting lots.
-LUKE 23:34

PEOPLE KNOW/DON'T REALLY KNOW WHAT THEY DO

Let me paint the picture. Jesus was literally hanging on the cross while the Roman soldiers were rolling dice for His clothes. These men had literally driven nails through Jesus' hands and feet, lifted up the cross and were gambling for His tunic, all in front of Him while He was slowly dying the slowest and most painful death that the Roman government could create. So, on one hand, they were 100% conscience of their actions and were seemingly enjoying their game of rolling dice to see who would get Jesus' tunic. But on the other hand, they were clueless to the fact that they were personally responsible for the torture and death of a completely innocent man. They treated their cruelty like sport to be enjoyed. Intellectually, they chose their actions, but they did not have the conscience to understand how cruel they were to an innocent man.

FORGIVENESS, LIKE HEALING, CAN TAKE TIME

Because God teaches forgiveness, some people and pastors place a demand on people to forgive instantly. This is not healthy, nor is it possible at times. There may be a measure of healing and regaining strength before forgiveness can be granted. It cannot be forced, it must be a conscious choice. If you have not received God's forgiveness yet, it will be even harder to offer forgiveness because you probably don't have any reference point.

BACK TO THE HEALING PROCESS

What matters most is that you begin a healing process. To the degree you can, cut off the source of pain. Begin to share your pain with both God and people. Talk about it, pray about it. Let God and people help you. God made us in such a way that we need Him, and we need people. God will also help you avoid people who tear down and connect you with people who will build you up. Use all the resources you need. It may be a pastor, counselor and many others. Who is your team? Surround yourself with people who want to see you win. I have learned that God will give you people who want nothing from you, but only to see you become all that He created you to be. In order to be all that God has created you to be, you have to heal and be made whole. Just like being torn down or broken is a process, so is healing and becoming whole.

I can't tell you exactly what you need, but if you start the process, ask God to lead you, and surround yourself with the right people, you will learn what you need to do. I had no idea how to heal when I began, but God has led me and connected me with great people. It may be hard for you to believe right now, but there are good people out there who will help you. Keep learning and ask God to help you along the way. The sooner you start the process of healing and the more focused and committed you are, the faster your progress will be.

CHAPTER 17

GRIEVING LOSS

Grieving is a process that few people ever think about. It is a process when a person feels or realizes a significant loss in their life. It is a demonstration of an emotionally healthy person acknowledging the reality of loss. It can also be magnified by past hurts, multiple losses, and current stress a person is going through. Grief is very real and is different for every person.

People often don't know the importance of or how to grieve, but grieving is healthy. Grieving acknowledges the reality that we lost something or never received it at all. It is the needed process of letting go of the pain of loss. I had to grieve growing up without my father, and then I had to grieve who my father was when I found him. I still grieve the man he never became. Later, when he passed away, I had to grieve that though he was broken, he was gone, and I wish I still had him.

GRIEF IS A PROCESS

Grieving can be looked at as a process or even a season. There are things we can do to help this process or like many people, we just walk through it. Grief is one of those things that people just don't talk about. Most of us have never even thought about the process. One thing I learned about grief is that it can't be rushed. It is what it is. Like making a tray of lasagna, it takes a lot of time, is best when left sitting overnight and baked the next day. If you try to speed up the process by cooking immediately, you will get lasagna, but it won't be as good. If you skip steps or try to microwave it, you will get something, but not what you wanted.

Grieving is also an individual experience. My father had 8 children and that means there are 8 different grieving processes, because we are all going through different levels of pain. I may have less pain because of the time I spent with my father. Others may have more pain because they didn't have that opportunity. Still, others may not have as much pain because they disconnected long ago and didn't have strong positive emotions towards him. I am speculating on these matters, but they are all possibilities, and no one knows how a person feels except themselves.

GRIEF IF A BROKEN HEART, NOT A BROKEN MIND

Throughout their book *The Grief Recovery Handbook*, James and Friedman, discuss that grief is a broken heart, not a broken mind.[21] What this means is that grief is something that is emotional, and it can't be solved or answered. This is important to know because many people give us intellectual answers and reasoning in an attempt to help us, but it's often the wrong medicine. For me, I was hurting, and people would tell me it was good that I spent the last days of my dad's life with him. Their comments were correct, and they meant well, but comments like this actually brought pain instead of comfort. People often don't know what to say when there is loss, especially when it is unexpected.

MY GRIEF CAME IN STAGES

When my father died, everything started happening so fast. We were on a family vacation. All of a sudden, my father was gone, and we had to make arrangements to transport the body and plan all of the funeral arrangements. One of my first stages was anger. I was angry because we had spoken many times about him putting his affairs in order for the day he did pass, but he always avoided the conversation and took no action. So, when he passed away, I was the one left to clean up his mess and I became very angry. I tried to avoid this very situation and now it was mine to deal with.

DEPRESSION CAME NEXT

Many people misunderstand depression and even see it as a sign of weakness, but this is mistaken. Depression is often the physical response to a loss or traumatic situation that can either be short or long term. So, for about two months I experienced deep depression and fear. This was a very dark place that I had never experienced before or after his death. Depression comes from being overwhelmed by emotions that we don't know how to navigate. I believe it was the trauma of watching my father die. My mind kept going back to the feeling of helplessness. I would have done anything to save my father, but I was powerless to do anything.

COUNSELING HELPED MY PROCESS MY EMOTIONS

Feelings of depression and fear often result from an inability to handle overwhelming emotions or life circumstances. I knew I needed help. Many individuals and groups of people have a stigma against counseling. This is not good. It is often socially unacceptable to admit to inabilities in handling many other areas of life, but people will look down on you if you need emotional or mental help. For instance, there are very few people who I can call up and ask to run a marathon. Most people would laugh at me and tell me I was crazy, and they could never run a marathon. Even if they thought they could, they would want a lot of time, training and multiple coaches!

But when my father died in my arms, I was immediately asked to run an emotional marathon. To be the strong one for my mom, my twin sister and six of my half-siblings. For me, my counselor was like a coach to help me navigate, plan and overcome. I needed help and I am glad I got it. So many people suffer through the pain of loss and trauma by themselves when there are trained experts who can help them. Some are too proud, and others don't know they can get help. Just like there is nothing wrong with a person getting a coach to help them run a physical marathon, getting help from a counselor to coach you through a tough season may be exactly what you need.

DON'T LISTEN TO EVERY VOICE

One of the worst things was religious people and family members telling me how I was supposed to grieve. There are times when religious people just say ridiculous things and even misquote or misapply Bible passages. Some people were literally telling me to "get over it" while others simply couldn't understand what I saw and experienced. Family members also said different things that were not helpful as they were trying to process their own pain. Either way, you have to know what voices to listen to and when you need to get away from certain voices. You have to make yourself the priority when you are going through a tough time and not worry about people who either don't understand or don't know how to share love and wisdom.

I learned to process my own feelings and not listen to people who are not professional. Grief is a process and again, everyone grieves differently. Along the way, you will not understand all of your thoughts and emotions, but you have to keep moving through the process. Grieving is a journey, not a destination, and the main goal should be to come through on the other side emotionally and spiritually healthier than before. That has been my experience after losing my father. I had to go through this process to be refined and that has made me a better person and a more effective leader to others.

MY GRIEF WAS NOT WITHOUT HOPE

One of the greatest gifts of having a personal relationship with Jesus is that I have the hope of eternity. Though I miss my father, I have 100% hope and faith that I will be with him in heaven for eternity. Let's look again to God's Word to see where that hope comes from.

> *Brothers and sisters, we do not want you to be uninformed about those who sleep in death, so that you do not grieve like the rest of mankind, who have no hope. -1 THESSALONIANS 4:13*

This verse was written by the Apostle Paul to encourage people who were in the grieving process. He is contrasting the hope of those who have put their faith in Christ compared to other people. As flawed as my father was, he came to a place where he recognized his sinfulness, asked Christ to forgive his sins, and followed Him.

What separates us from God is our sin, but Christ died to pay the price for our sin on the cross, so that we could be forgiven and reconnected with God. Imagine someone commits a crime and they either have to do the time or pay some amount they could not afford, let's say 1 trillion dollars, but then someone comes along and can pay that amount. When that person pays it, the person who committed the crime can go free. Sin is basically crime against people, but even worse, against God. Thankfully, God loves us so much that He sent His Son Jesus to die on the cross to pay the sin penalty in our place. He then offers this as a gift to us.

WHY THE JESUS FOCUS?

Some of you reading this book may come from different faiths or no faith at all and may ask why I focus so much on Jesus. As a Christian, I see Christianity as having a personal relationship with Jesus. Many ask about other religious leaders and philosophers. While just about all religious leaders and philosophers have positive moral teaching and guidance, Jesus is fundamentally different in that He literally died for our sins, removing the very thing that stands to separate us from God. No one else died to pay the price for our sins so no one else can give us eternal life. Christians are no better than anyone else; they have simply learned God's plan and received Jesus as Lord and Savior.

THE GIFT OF GOD IS ETERNAL LIFE

For it is by grace you have been saved, through faith—and this is not from yourselves, it is the gift of God—not by works, so that no one can boast. -EPHESIANS 2:8-9

The word grace in this verse means "unmerited favor" or simply God showing His love and favor to someone who hasn't earned it. In fact, it is impossible to be good enough to earn eternal life with God.

This forgiveness is received through faith. When I put my faith in what Jesus did on the cross, He came into my heart, washed away all my sin and became both my Lord and my Savior. Savior in the sense that He took away my sin penalty, and Lord in that I chose to follow His leading in my life instead of my own flesh and what the world kept pushing me to do. This is the same experience my father had. When both of us chose to let Jesus lead our lives, that is when God brought us back together. Before that, we were both walking away from God and from each other.

Many would say neither me nor my father deserved this type of forgiveness and acceptance from God, and they would be correct. Grace means God giving us better than we deserve because He is the loving Father. This is "not of yourselves" which means we did not and could not earn these things. We can't brag about how good we are, that's for sure, but God still had a plan for both of us even when we were very rebellious toward Him.

GRIEVING IS TEMPORARY

Grieving is a temporary process in this life and non-existent in heaven. Grieving also comes in waves and seasons. Like any traumatic experience, certain things will trigger grief. I remember the first time I went hiking in Lake George. I actually went on a couple of hikes over several days. It brought me both pain and joy because it reminded me of the hike with my father. I thought back on the wonderful moments that God gave me with my father while also feeling the pain of him being gone. Yes, I have faith that I will see him again and be with him for all eternity, but I also miss him at times.

So, I grieved and rejoiced as I climbed up and down mountains thousands of miles from where I hiked with my dad. It helped me to let go of some of my pain and taught me to hold on to the good memories, even about that hike. I also look forward to heaven which is eternity with God and eternity with the people that have received Jesus as their Lord and Savior. Let's take a look at a quick picture of heaven.

He will wipe every tear from their eyes. There will be no more
death or mourning or crying or pain, for the old order of things has
passed away. -REVELATION 21:4

So, in heaven, God will wipe away every tear. There will be no more death and loss because in heaven, things are better, and things are different. On this side of eternity, I will probably always miss my father and have regrets from time to time, but God continues to heal me as I walk with Him. I also have great hope and encouragement that the day will come when this grief and sorrow will be gone.

CHAPTER 18

PROCESSING MY ANGER

I had to make a choice between letting my anger
make me bitter or better.

-JACK REDMOND

I was angry. At some point, I was probably angry with everyone. I was angry because of the things I experienced, angry at God, my dad, mom, step-dad and very angry at myself. Throw in friends, several of my ex's, society, the world... I think you get the idea. The question is "what do you do with this anger?" You can say what you want about anger, but when it's present, you have to figure out what to do with it.

People often look at anger as a bad thing, and it can be. But, anger is actually a healthy response to injustice or when someone hurts you. What we do with anger is another story. I had to allow my anger to do two things. First, to motivate me to be a better person and not to repeat generational destructive behaviors. Secondly, to confront my father and others about things that they were doing wrong. I didn't always handle it well. After an incident where I choked my father and another time when I had a physical fight with my 25-year-old son, I had to revisit my anger and commit to further healing so I could handle it better. Though my anger was justified, my actions were absolutely wrong. I had to choose to let my anger drive me to be better, otherwise it would just create more damage and pain for me, my son and those that followed.

MEN HAVE A TENDENCY TOWARDS ANGER

When men are faced with disappointment, chaos or confrontation, the natural reaction tends to be anger. Women, when faced with similar situations, may tend to become upset or sad. Both men and women feel and react in both ways, but men tend to flow towards anger. Part of this is physiological. Men have more testosterone which is needed in combat, hard physical exertion, etc. We can see how men have fought wars, hunted for survival and done great works which is in some part powered by this and other physiological aspects. I had to learn to put my anger in God's hands so that it would result in positive change, not more destruction and pain.

LETTING GOD DIRECT MY ANGER

"In your anger do not sin": Do not let the sun go down while you are still angry... -EPHESIANS 4:26

Most people don't even know that the Bible teaches on things like anger management! This verse is not telling us to never be angry, but when we are angry, we should be mindful not to sin. Remember that sin is anything outside of the will of God. The Bible is teaching us that when we get angry, we should not allow the anger to drive us to do things considered damaging or destructive.

I had a right to be angry at my father for all he did and didn't do. He neglected me, then when he came back in my life, he used me and lied to me! My dad, who told everyone he had all kinds of land and money that he didn't, showed up at my doorstep with no place to live.

I took him in and gave him a place to stay, but we agreed that he would have to pay rent. At some point, he wasn't paying the full amount and when I confronted him about it, he lied to me. He looked me directly in the face and lied about the amount we had agreed to. When I confronted him, he went into street mode, kept lying and then turned everything against me and started accusing me of things. At some point, I snapped and grabbed him, took him to the ground, and literally choked him. I am ashamed that I did that. My anger was justified, but my actions were wrong.

With my son, I also lost my anger. This was also due to a feeling of injustice. I became a father at the age of 19. Unlike my father, I took the responsibility of raising my son very seriously. I arranged my life so that he could be with me. I changed my lifestyle, worked hard and gave him many things my father never gave me. I was physically, emotionally and financially responsible and present. Like many boys, at some point, he was unappreciative and disrespectful to me. Once, it got so heated that we actually fought. The anger overtook me. I was justified in my anger based on the actions and feelings of my son, but my actions were wrong, and I knew I needed to change.

Many men also take out their anger on their wives/girlfriends, their children and on others. I am no better than them, but abusive actions towards children are even worse and never acceptable. Even though, I have not done these things, I can see how they happen. Unresolved bitterness and anger can come out against anyone, both verbally and physically. This is a reality that often goes unaddressed.

GETTING PROFESSIONAL HELP TO DEAL WITH ANGER

Anger by itself is not the problem, it is an improper response to anger that hurts people. Anger is one of the things that time alone will not heal. When a person has been damaged over time, they can be like a wounded animal striking out at others, even those who are trying to help them. People seek help for so many problems but seeking help for things like anger are taboo for many. Because issues like this are taboo, people don't want to even talk about it, never mind schedule and show up for a series of appointments! But you don't need to feel this way. Counselors deal with anger and many other issues every day. Things that you may feel no one is talking about, are being talked about every day by experts who are helping people. I encourage you to not be fearful about getting help. I also encourage you to not be too proud to get help. If you had a physical wound, you would go to the emergency room and then to proper treatment or rehabilitation until you were better, so why would you not get the emotional help and treatment that you need to be strong and healthy? I also had to be humble if I didn't want my son and future grandchildren to repeat the same mistakes I made.

FOCUS ANGER ON PROBLEMS, NOT PEOPLE

It is wise to direct your anger towards problems — not people;
to focus your energies on answers — not excuses.
-WILLIAM ARTHUR WARD[22]

I had to direct my anger towards my problems and my brokenness. When I focused on my dad and son, I lashed out in anger. Even though I was not physically aggressive towards women at that point of my life, when there were problems, I would lash out verbally or leave. You see, leaving a woman just because of anger is hurtful and damaging, and we think it's ok because it's emotional damage and not physical.

First, I had to get help in understanding and navigating who I had become. Remember that broken little boy was now in a 6 foot 3, 220-pound body. Before I could expect to help anyone else, I had to help myself. I learned that we must deal with problems from a place of strength, not a place of weakness or brokenness. As I learned about myself, it also helped me understand why others behaved and reacted the way they did.

I realized that my dad had probably been in the same situations I was in, but never knew how to stop, call a time out and get the help he needed. This scared me because it also showed me the road I was on. I needed to take a detour, get strong and choose a new direction for my life.

FOCUSING ON PEOPLE'S PROBLEMS AND NOT THEIR BEHAVIORS

The next step was looking at my dad, son and others through different lenses. I had been looking at their behaviors. Like a wounded animal, they were striking out at me when I was trying to help them. I learned to begin to first try to help others to become whole and healed. When I focus on the problems, I also view the person differently. My emotions are directed to overcoming a problem, not fixing a person I am angry with.

During that process, we connected in deeper ways which made it easier to address issues in a real way. If you want people's behaviors to change, you have to get to the root of what is driving them. If neglect, pain, abuse, disappointment and other things are driving them, you may be able to get them to change behaviors temporarily, but the same issues will come back when under stress. I was also able to model new behaviors to both my father and son to help them also see that change is possible.

I HAD TO STOP MAKING EXCUSES!

Lastly, by focusing on personal problems, it can cause people to seek answers and stop settling for excuses. I had to stop making excuses for my lack of commitment towards women. The problem was me. I was too immature to value and commit to a single woman. This was my character flaw and weakness. I had to stop making excuses about my unfaithfulness and lack of commitment being "normal." Me being a weak man, unable to commit and walk through tough times was my issue and I needed to confront myself.

I had to realize that what my father did or did not do was not my main issue. I had to decide what I was going to do. It didn't matter what all my peers were doing, I had to do the right things before God, myself and those in my life. There are always reasons for what people do, but it doesn't make things right.

BECOMING BETTER, NOT BITTER

Life will make you bitter if you let it! But, bitterness eats away at your soul, drives you to medicate with drugs, alcohol or sex and to hide from real life. Bitterness makes you feel overwhelmed to the point where you justify self-destructive behaviors and treating others badly. It is by committing to growth and healing that you become better. Remember the prayer: *"God, what do I do with this?"* I think another way of saying this is, *"God, how do I let my pain make me better?"* God is not the author of our pain, but we can let Him re-write our lives to make us better instead of bitter.

CHAPTER 19

WISHING FOR ONE MORE DAY

My last memories of my dad were on a mountain in Hawaii as the family went on a hike. We had no warning or idea that our family dream was about to turn into a nightmare. As we hiked and laughed, suddenly I heard my two sisters screaming. I ran to them to see my father gasping for breath, collapsed on the ground. Eventually the medics came and began CPR but were doing it wrong. I pushed them out of the way and began giving my father CPR. He continued to fade, but his last breath was a gush of air that he breathed into my lungs.

CELEBRATING AS A FAMILY

My sister's son just graduated high school in Hawaii. This was also an opportunity for some of our family to spend time together on the beautiful island. In many ways, this time together was a dream come true. A portion of my family was together, and I was with my dad. Up until this point, my father was strong and healthy. We went on a hike in paradise. I don't know many people who have ever had the opportunity to enjoy the sights we saw that day. We laughed, just enjoying the day with no pressure, spending time together as a family. God had answered my prayers and reunited me with my father and began a healing process. It was not always smooth, but it was good.

Growing up, I never played catch with my dad and he never came to a basketball game to cheer me on, but now we were together. Hawaii was different; three days before the hike, my dad and I spent a day together at the beach. We played in the ocean like two little kids. It was special for both of us. Although other family members were with us, this day was all about me and my dad. We played for hours in the water. It even started raining, but we did not care. This day was about me and my dad bonding like father and son. Just as the other fun was helping, this hike was the type of thing that was filling in gaps and helping me heal. Even as flawed as my father was, he was a lot of fun to be around.

Things had gotten so much better. My father had been living with me. We had been putting the family back together, piece by piece. We were in Hawaii to celebrate my nephew's high school graduation along with some of the family. It was like a dream come true. We shared a house and were spending good times together, until my father's heart attack.

MY FATHER COLLAPSED

He was strong and vibrant, and his collapse came out of nowhere. It was somewhat strenuous going up the hill, but it wasn't a dangerous level of activity. It was not like he had ongoing heart issues that would have kept him from taking a hike like this. It was a beautiful time in a beautiful place.

Pain, fear and shock ran through me as I realized that my father was gone. My dream became an instant nightmare. So many hopes had been fulfilled, but now so many hopes would never be fulfilled.

Over the next weeks and months thankfulness and regret, gratefulness and anger, battled within me. I had my dad back and now he was gone. Over the years, I had loved him and hated him. I prayed to see him at times, and at others, wished I would never see him again. I was reunited with him and now he was gone. I'm sure my siblings had many and even more of these feelings.

MEETING THE REST OF MY FAMILY

The first time all my brothers and sisters were together was at my father's funeral. My father had eight children by six different women. Some of the brothers and sisters met for the first time. This was also the first time we had to plan or do anything together. This time further demonstrated both the good and the bad my father had done. So many good qualities were mixed in with so much pain. I was able to see how the same type of questions and emotions were present in my half siblings. For the most part, things went well but there were obvious areas of brokenness that came out that we didn't really have time to deal with before or during the funeral.

MY CHURCH FAMILY SHOWED UP

Over time, my church family had also become my family. During and after the funeral, their support helped me through. People showed up to pray, encourage and just to serve. This time strengthened existing friendships and caused new ones to begin. I appreciate friends I grew up with, went to college with and others I connected with along the way, but there is something special about my brothers and sisters in Christ. Our relationship with Jesus helps us to be united in heart. They also have an understanding of both the present and eternity. They walked with me through the reality and pain I was in, and also encouraged me to lean on God for His strength because He can help us in ways that no human can.

MY DAD'S LAST BREATH

Most things my dad did were a mixture of good and bad. In some ways, this was a spiritual experience as the man who gave me life, breathed his last breath into my lungs. It was a deeply powerful experience. It was like a powerful gush of air, as his last physical act was giving me his very breath. I considered this an honor and gift from God.

The bad side was that part of this breath was somehow toxic to me. It actually affected my lungs for the next several weeks. I physically felt sick. Then a time came when I was going through the mourning process and was in a time of prayer where I actually coughed up and physically vomited until my lungs felt clear and I felt healthy again.

This is an example of what I mean by holding onto the good and letting go of the bad of a person. On one hand, I thanked God for the honor of receiving my father's last breath and would keep the good, while also seeing the need and healthiness of getting rid of the toxic part I had received. This amazes me as this paints a picture of my dad's influence in my life. I continue to learn to receive from my dad's goodness while overcoming and leaving certain things behind and moving forward. I said good bye to my father on a mountain side in Hawaii, but deep down, I wish I could be with him for just one more day.

SECTION 5

For the Ladies

CHAPTER 20

LEARNING TO LOVE

IF

Only if you would have come with instructions,
Fragile handle with care DEAR,

And if I would have KNOWN how EMOTIONAL you
Really WERE

And Only IF I would have been taught more
Patience and Kindness,

And IF I wasn't so Insecure,

And, IF, and Only If, I did not insist on my way and
Wanted so much CONTROL,

And, Maybe IF I would have known how to trust,
and Believe in YOU,

And, IF, I only had one clue that SEX,
Was more than a PHYSICAL act and

Your HEART was involved TOO,

Then, maybe just Maybe,
I would have known how to
LOVE YOU A WOMAN!

I not only missed being loved by my father, I missed out on the life lessons of learning how to love others, especially women. The reality is that we do what we know, and this comes from what we are taught, as well as our environment. Some things are taught, others are caught. I had strong feelings, but looking back, healthy love was not there. My brand of love was driven by feelings of lust, but it was not true love. Some of these things I learned while others were caught because that's what my environment taught me. To change, first I had to learn that God loves me, then I had to learn to love myself, and then I learned to love others. This is a process I'm still growing in. Most people have never thought about learning to love better. This is key for men if they want to be good husbands and fathers.

One of my favorite Bible passages describes how God defines love.

Love is patient, love is kind.
It does not envy, it does not boast, it is not proud.
It does not dishonor others, it is not self-seeking,
it is not easily angered, it keeps no record of wrongs.
Love does not delight in evil but rejoices with the truth.
It always protects, always trusts, always hopes, always perseveres.
Love never fails.
And now these three remain: faith, hope and love.
But the greatest of these is love.
-1 CORINTHIANS 13:4-8;13

I NEEDED TO DO A U-TURN

My brand of love was the exact opposite of God's love. My love was impatient, unkind, jealous, proud and boastful! I sought after what I wanted, was easily angered and remembered every wrong word or action and made sure I used it against people and to my advantage. Though I wasn't purposely being evil, I was deliberately doing things that were deceitful and hurtful. I lied, never trusted, had no hope the relationship would last and was always looking to move on to my next conquest quickly. God's love may as well have been from a different planet than mine, well, actually it does come from a different place and a better place. I had much to learn.

TRUE LOVE WAS A FOREIGN LANGUAGE TO ME

In the Fall of 2017 I was part of a 10-man team that went to Managua, Nicaragua with the goal of training men to be better husbands and fathers. This reality was magnified as we were also working with a group of 30 teen girls who had been rescued from prostitution, so we were literally fighting the forces that drove these young girls into that horrible lifestyle. We met with a group of local workers and their wives and then a group of pastors and their wives to bring them through a program they would later share with their congregations.

One small interesting fact – I don't speak Spanish. So, I was thrust into an environment where I literally did not have the ability to communicate with the people I went to serve. I couldn't speak in a way they could understand, and I had no idea what people were saying when they asked questions or wanted to tell me something.

I NEEDED A TRANSLATOR

If I wanted to effectively communicate and serve these wonderful people, I needed a translator. I needed someone who knew the language, could understand me and help me communicate back and forth. My translator had to know more than me and care about me enough to help me. Yes, I could learn Spanish, but that would probably take years and I needed help immediately for our time in Nicaragua. So, what does not being able to speak Spanish and loving people have in common?

At some point, I realized that I did not know what clean, healthy, godly love was. This was different because what I knew about love, I learned from my surroundings, so I thought what I knew was normal and correct. But, when I was immersed in a Spanish culture, it was clear I needed a translator.

When I became a Christian, all of a sudden, I was in a new place spiritually where it became evident that I didn't speak God's language of love. Jesus became my translator. I began to look at His life as a model and my teaching tool to see what true, wholesome, sacrificial love looked like. He then became my coach, guiding me in my interactions with people. Just like learning Spanish requires a new type of thinking, Jesus began to teach me to think differently about love. My thinking had to change from taking to giving, from being served to serving and from being self-absorbed and greedy to being focused on others and generous.

GOD IS LOVE

To learn how to love, I had to go to the author of love. In life, the best and most valuable things are often in their purest form. Think about it. Pure gold is much more valuable than gold mixed with other metals. Pure love is much more valuable than partial love. God is the only one whose love is 100% pure. So, going to God to learn about love is the best choice.

Whoever does not love does not know God, because God is love.
-1 JOHN 4:8

I lived this scripture. I did not know God, so I did not know love. I knew religion, I knew right and wrong and I understood morality even though I constantly contradicted good morals. But since I did not know and understand God, I did not love. Just like I did not know or understand Spanish, I could not communicate in Spanish. Though I was very intelligent and successful in many areas, I was not successful in loving people in a healthy way. Keep in mind, everyone looking at me would have considered me "successful" in my relationships. I could easily begin and maintain relationships with people when I wanted to, but they were not based on love.

The Bible teaches us that God is not just an example of love or that God is loving, but that God actually is love. This means God's DNA is love. It's not only what God does, but who God is! So, by getting to know God, you get to know love. If you have not yet had this experience, this may seem different or either strange compared to your current understanding of God, but it doesn't change who God is. I pray that you will have this personal experience for yourself. God's love is so much bigger than the limited religious experiences that many people have had. I encourage you to get to know God so that you can truly understand pure love.

MEN OF GOD DEMONSTRATED TRUE LOVE

In addition to God, I learned that I must learn to receive love from people who wanted nothing from me but only to be a blessing to me. God created us to be relational and certain things we must learn through our interactions with people. I learned this from other men in my church. Men in my church began to love me as a son and brother. Unfortunately, many people use "love" to get what they want. I had always used "love" this way. Thankfully, I also learned through my pastors and other men in my church to love God, love myself and then to love a woman in a healthy way. This type of love was revolutionary in my life! This type of love is life building.

LEARNING THAT LOVE WAS NOT A SEXUAL THING

I also learned to purposely reject many of the ideas and beliefs that I had if I wanted to replace them with healthier ones. For decades, my dominant idea of "love" meant a feeling I had towards someone that I wanted to have sex with. I also had a form of love, that was for family and maybe friends, but in my priorities, these were secondary feelings different than what I connected with romance and sex. In short, I did not know how to love anyone in a pure and godly way.

I HAD TO LEARN TO LOVE WOMEN IN A HEALTHY WAY

I had to learn that love protects and provides. This was totally different than my version of love which was selfish and all about using and taking, not protecting and providing. I had to learn to value women as precious, not as consumable products. Remember, God's Word teaches us that God wants to renew our minds. I experienced God changing the way I thought about love and women. The result of this: I have now been faithfully married for the past seven years.

If you would have told me this was possible before I started following Jesus, I would have laughed at you. Though I wanted a fulfilling life-long marriage, I didn't even know if that was possible or how to have one. First, God changed my heart and mind, then men helped me walk it out.

NOTE TO WOMEN

Many women have been hurt by men like me, men who are unable to love a woman properly because of their lack of understanding and brokenness. So many women have blamed themselves for not being lovable because they had expected a man to do something that they are incapable of doing. Many women who desire love, commitment and marriage have put their hope in a man who has no idea of how to properly love a woman. These are all good and healthy desires, but many times, women are dealing with the wrong type of guy and many lack a relationship with Jesus needed to understand love and their true worth, so they settle or many don't even know there are better options.

Without a relationship with Jesus and the support of godly men, men will not have the proper view or even desire to give the love a woman both needs and desires. They are looking at women and life through the wrong lenses and don't know the true language of love that comes from God.

I want to be clear, I am not talking about a man who just "believes in God," I am talking about a man who has surrendered his life to Jesus and is committed to living by His Word and being led by the Holy Spirit. This type of man is in relationship with Jesus in such a way that Jesus is shaping and molding him on a daily basis. If Jesus is not shaping and molding your man, you will be the one trying to shape and mold him. I hear this tired story every week, if not daily, of good women trying to change a man who doesn't want to change. Yes, woman have positive influences on men, but no person can replace the work of God in a man's life.

I want to be very clear to you. If you have tried to change a man and it has not been successful, you are not a failure! You tried to do work that only God can do, and since you are not God, you can't change a person. Please don't beat yourself up if this has been your experience. So many women have felt and even been told by broken men that they are not good enough. Understand that this is a lie. You are good enough; unfortunately, you put your hope in a man or men that don't have the ability to be who you want them to be without God.

So, women, first priority is that you have a personal relationship with Jesus and let God bring you together with a man who also is a passionate follower of Jesus. Then God will weave your lives together as you both continue to be shaped and molded through God's own love.

CHAPTER 21

FATHERLESS DAUGHTERS

When we set out to write this book, our focus was on men and helping them overcome the brokenness when they are raised with an absent or ineffective father. But, as we wrote, there were so many times when we felt so strongly about the value and goodness of women, that we wanted to write this last section in honor of the women in our lives and also to help women understand some things about men. We also recognize that many women have held families together and raised children when men have failed and not been present. Women also have suffered from a lack of fathering, and we want to both honor and help women who are a tremendous blessing to all of mankind.

In the same way that young men receive certain things from their fathers, there are also specific things that only a father can give to a daughter. Once again, this doesn't take anything away from a mother's role or importance, it is just saying that each have unique things to give. It's like being in school where a Chemistry teacher knows things an English teacher doesn't and vice versa. They are experts in what they do and have input the other one doesn't. They are both important, just different. Only a man can give proper male affection. Usually a mother is more affectionate and will actually give more affection to a daughter, but they cannot give proper male affection which meets certain needs and provides a reference point later on in life.

Fathers are meant to help their daughters establish their personal worth, provide a sense of security and teach them how to interact with the opposite sex. When a father is absent, many young women may not understand healthy male-female relationships or may lack self-confidence and self-esteem. This can open the door to unwise decisions and lifestyles that are unhealthy. Many women who grow up without a dad turn out very well, but the reality is that many don't. Without a father to love and protect a daughter, the reality is that there are many more obstacles and pitfalls to navigate through and around. Unmet needs can also cause a young woman to look to another man to fill in gaps left from her father not being there.

A FATHER'S JOB IS TO PROTECT HIS DAUGHTER

Love does two things; it protects, and it provides. It's simple, if a boy shows up at a girl's house and the father greets him at the door, there is a totally different dynamic. The fact that a strong man is present changes the whole atmosphere. If that father is loving and protective, that will chase away a whole lot of jokers. It also sets the tone for proper interactions as opposed to some boy just trying to get some.

Then, if a boy starts acting stupid or like he has some type of sexual rights with the girl, a father is there to help his daughter navigate this and also stand strong. How many young girls have been attracted to an older man because of an emotional need that a man then uses to move into a sexual relationship. The young girl wanted affirmation and at some point, the game changed; in order to hear the words of affirmation, she must give up sex. Yes, this can be mutual and wanted by the girl, but how many young women have been encouraged to engage in sex before they had actually planned or wanted to?

FATHER AS PROVIDER

As a young girl growing up, it is a father's job to provide a safe and loving atmosphere for his daughter's growth. The father is also there to give love and healthy affection. A young girl who grows up being told she is beautiful and gets many hugs along the way will generally have a much stronger self-esteem and will not have an empty soul because her father filled it with love. In recent years, there has been a lot of talk about people and their emotional tanks. One of the father's responsibilities is to help fill up his daughter's emotional tank.

If this same man demonstrates love and affection to this girl's mother, she will develop a standard and expectation of how she deserves to be treated. Then, if that standard is not met, she will know that something is wrong. The reality is also that she will carry herself in such a way that a young man who just wants his way will most likely think twice when he sees a strong young women and will move on to easier prey.

A father's role is also to provide financially. When a child grows up without having to worry about food and basic life needs, they are able to focus on flourishing. A father who provides financially helps his daughter have a healthy mindset, having high personal standards, goal setting and support to get there. Many women talk about how they felt safe or comfortable when their father was home. His presence brought reassurance. A father's presence also provides stability and routine in a child's life, which also positions them for success. Call it what you want to call it, but money makes a difference and a stable income is a blessing to a child.

An absent father creates a gap emotionally and practically in so many ways. It can also lead to low expectations of never having or achieving much. Others are driven the other way to excel and this can be both good and bad. Good because young girls can be hungry to work hard, get a great education and do well. It can also have a bad side effect of becoming overly self-reliant in a way that may push men away. There is nothing wrong with being self-reliant and that can be needed, but sometimes, it can lead to being so focused that women miss out on things that they actually want, like getting married and having a family of their own.

THE "YOU DON'T NEED A MAN" MINDSET

Some single mothers, especially those who have been treated badly and have had to learn how to survive on their own, without the father of their child or children, can have this mindset. Many of these women are amazing examples of strength who do a great job as a mother. Please understand, I am not saying that a woman "needs a man" to be complete or to be successful. What I am saying is that it is optimal for a child to have two loving parents and receive from both a mother and a father. And yes, you can find many examples of children being raised better by a single mom than children in a two-parent home. I have much respect for single mothers, but also acknowledge the challenges it presents. One of the downsides is often in their pain; some women project an image of men that is negative and then promote their daughters to be "independent" in an unhealthy way making them believe they will never need a man. There are also some women that are straight up toxic towards men due to the pain men have caused, but this can keep them from the healthy relationship they desire.

While I absolutely believe in today's world and economy in which women need to be educated, focused and able to make money to either support themselves while single or in their family with their husband when married, there can be some negatives if this is taken too far. What do I mean by this? Some women who grow up without a father are raised in an atmosphere where men are portrayed poorly and where there is such a strong drive to be self-sufficient that eventually when a woman wants to be married, she can be abrasive and unattractive to men. Other women are so focused on success that they wake up at 35 years old and look around and don't see many men left that they would want to marry!

It pains my heart when I see incredibly successful, beautiful women who want to get married and can't understand why they can't meet the husband of their dreams. I am not saying a woman must be married or that a woman needs to depend on a man, but what I am saying is that some women have been raised and embrace an attitude that hurts them in terms of either marrying much later than they wanted, or not at all. Yes, it is true that some men do not want a strong woman. But many men do, and they also want a woman who can be feminine and soft at times. This can be hard for women who did not grow up in an atmosphere where both strength and femininity were encouraged.

UNDERSTAND THE GAPS AND FEED THEM

As a man, I can't speak to women's experiences, needs and issues in the same way that I can speak to men's experiences, but some of the principles still apply. If there have been gaps of experience and learning, they should be identified. In our church, many of the older couples make it a point to help young women. Many men act as spiritual fathers who express healthy interactions in a fatherly way. It is also important for women to see what healthy marriages and interactions look like.

In the same way that a person can be nutritionally malnourished, a person can be emotionally and experience malnourished. If a person is anemic, they will need more iron. They are not bad because they have a deficiency, they just need to learn what that deficiency is and make sure they get that extra nourishment. If those unmet needs are not dealt with, you will not flourish and may pass on the same deficiencies to your children.

WHEN FATHERLESS GIRLS MEET FATHERLESS BOYS

People tend to gravitate towards others with similar experiences. For instance, people who grew up in stable loving families tend to marry others who grew up in a similar situation. People recognize and feel comfortable with familiarity. The tendency is also the same for people who grow up in single mother households; they are more likely to get involved with people who grew up in similar situations. This isn't a hard, fast rule but tends to be that way. This was how it was growing up for me. Guys dating girls with all kinds of emotional gaps and used to seeing and accepting all kinds of things.

When you have two people get married who both have large gaps from their upbringing, this will require both people to work harder to make things work. Many of the girls I dated expected me to cheat or leave at some point. This is very unhealthy, but many people embrace this thinking because they feel like they have no choice. This allows dysfunction to continue. If you want something different, you need to do something different!

GO TO GOD FIRST

Just like I talked about my need to go to God as my Father and provider, the same applies to you. Let Him teach you about pure and faithful love and how to seek and yes, demand pure love from others. You are worth it, and you will get what you either demand or settle for! Also, let God heal you. I don't like using words like "toxic" to describe someone, especially when they have been neglected, deserted or abused, but I have met women that look me in the face and declare "Oh yeah, I am toxic!" They didn't say this from a place of pride, but from a place where they were asking for help because they had been emotionally destroyed over the years. I have seen God give these women peace as He healed them and helped them move forward.

THERE AREN'T A LOT OF GOOD MEN AROUND

I'm not going to argue with you on this, but instead tell you one simple fact to encourage you. You don't need a lot of good men, you only need one good man. If you go to God and focus on Him, God's Word teaches us that He will give you what you desire. Grow in your relationship with God and keep growing every day. Don't settle, but also don't be so picky that no one is good enough. First, you don't need to settle, that's not what God wants you to do. You don't need a perfect man, you just need the man that God has for you.

Let me be really simple, if a man wants you, he will come after you. A real man is not passive and can't be convinced to take something he doesn't really want. Also, if a man won't chase after you when you are single, that man will not chase after you when you are married. Women desire to be wanted and pursued, and men pursue what they want.

IT'S NOT ALL ABOUT LOOKS EITHER

Yes, society does overemphasize looks, but there are many women who are less than beautiful, who have a man and many gorgeous women who don't have a man; so, it's not all about looks. Shallow dating may be all about looks or sex, but true love is driven by much more. This is also why you want to put God first so that you will find a man who puts God first. That is the type of man that God will then lead to marry you, and then the marriage is not only a commitment to you, but a commitment to God. When both people are filled with God's love, their love will be a whole lot deeper than a surface attraction based on looks.

CHAPTER 22

WHY CAN'T I MAKE
MY MAN HAPPY?

Ladies on your own, you can't fix a man, you can't change a man,
and you can't heal a man. Sometimes, the only thing you can do
for a man is to pray for him and some men are so broken
that the only thing you can do is run the other way.

-MALIK CAREY

First thing – it is not your job or responsibility to make anyone happy!
True joy comes from God. If a person has that joy, other things will add to
them to bring happiness, but if someone doesn't have the joy of the Lord, it
is not up to a person to make someone happy. If you are doing everything
a man wants and he's not happy, the problem is not you. He's probably
broken and empty inside due to gaps left unfulfilled from many years ago.
So many women are trying to please a man who is unpleasable. I know this
because I was that man. When men have missing gaps that only a father
and God can fill, there is nothing a woman can do to fill them. A woman can meet many other physical and emotional needs, but deep unmet

needs will eventually scream so loud that most men will break up with a great woman because they know something is missing and blame the woman. Others will continue to chase after pleasure to numb the empty pain within. Trust me, the problem is not you.

GIVING YOUR BEST TO SOMEONE WHO CAN'T APPRECIATE

History is filled with wonderful women who have given their best to a man or men over time who literally did not have the ability to appreciate it. Here's what Jesus had to say about giving your best to those who either don't deserve or can't appreciate it.

Do not give dogs what is sacred; do not throw your pearls to pigs. If you do, they may trample them under their feet, and turn and tear you to pieces. -MATTHEW 7:6

Jesus is telling His followers that dogs can not appreciate sacred things. Imagine going to a fancy steakhouse and buying $100 steaks to feed your dog. The reality is that the dog may actually prefer a $2 can of dog food. Jesus then adds a second statement about not giving your pearls to pigs. When the Bible repeats a principle, it's to make an emphasis. So, don't give $100 steaks to dogs and don't take your precious pearls and throw them to pigs. Pigs don't know the difference between a precious pearl and a dirty rock. So, you can throw thousands of dollars' worth of pearls before pigs, and they will simply trample them and secondly, after you give away your best pearls to the pigs, they will turn on you and tear you to pieces. How many women have given their best to a man who doesn't appreciate it and then turns and hurts the woman?

Now, Jesus was not specifically addressing the issue of fatherlessness and the damage it causes but showing a principle that if you share your best with certain people, it will be meaningless to them and they will turn on you after you gave generously.

Jesus used the examples of dogs and pigs as examples of animals who lacked the capacity to appreciate things of value. I am not calling men dogs or pigs but let me speak for myself. Before I came to Jesus and went through a significant transformation, I literally did not have the ability to appreciate the value and efforts of women. I routinely took what was valuable and precious, consumed it, and did not understand its value or appreciate the efforts of women. At some point, it was my brokenness and at other times, it was my sin.

MEN WITH NO CONSCIENCE

Many people have lost the ability to feel or have a conscience for what they do. The Bible talks about people who have a "seared conscience" which means they do not feel. It is like a person who has been badly burned and when their skin heals, the nerves are dead and they have lost feeling. We may speak of people being "cold" and even promote when people are "gangster." Bottom line: many men don't feel or understand that they are hurting someone. Many men can't even feel.

This was me on the inside while I was smooth, attentive and even caring at times on the outside. This can be confusing because on one hand, a man can be kind, generous and very sincere, but once they enter into a different space, they can be cold, calculated and even ruthless. These bad traits also come out under stress, in conflict and unfortunately when someone doesn't get what they want when they want. Remember the chapter on the Adolescent Man? You can have tall, dark and handsome with an MBA and be dealing with an emotionally stunted 14-year-old, blaming yourself for their actions or inability to commit. It can be very hard to understand whether you are dealing with a hurting man, an immature and selfish man, or a man who is owned by sin.

I WAS A SLAVE TO SIN

If you are not familiar with the Bible, being a "slave to sin" may seem like a strange concept. Remember that sin can be roughly defined as anything outside of God's Will for our lives. This concept means that people are controlled by things outside of God's Will. My alcohol use, drug use, sleeping around, unhealthy desire and greed for money, being unfaithful to my girlfriends and first wife was all sin and it controlled my life. It didn't matter what any woman did for me, I needed Jesus to set me free.

But thanks be to God that, though you used to be slaves to sin, you have come to obey from your heart the pattern of teaching that has now claimed your allegiance. You have been set free from sin and have become slaves to righteousness. -ROMANS 6:17-18

Today, I can echo speak these words, "God, I thank you that I am free from the sin that controlled my life." I came to obey God from my heart and I learned from the Bible and my church. I was set free from slavery to sin to now being a "slave to righteousness." What this means is that now my life is controlled by doing the right things instead of the wrong. This all came from having a personal relationship with Jesus and following Him. This is key because God brought about the change that no person – man or woman could bring. Let me remind you to stop beating yourself up if you were unable to change a man; that's God's work and needs to be walked out with other men supporting, encouraging and holding them accountable. One more thought, if a man is not willing to be shaped by God, they will not be willing to be shaped by you or any other person!

WHY GOD SAYS BELIEVERS SHOULD BE WITH BELIEVERS

Let me share a very important principle when it comes to dating or marriage. God is very clear; He states that one of the key factors is that a couple should have the same faith system. The Bible uses the words "believer" and "unbelievers" meaning those who believe in Jesus as Lord and Savior and are committed to following the Bible vs. those who are not. This goes beyond going to church or someone who "believes in God" which are good actions and beliefs, but by themselves, don't mean a person is actually committed to following Jesus, being led by God and living by God's Word. It is very clear; God does not want us to be intimately woven together with people of different faith and intellectual places. Here is a verse that explains this.

Do not be yoked together with unbelievers. For what do righteous-
ness and wickedness have in common? Or what fellowship can light
have with darkness? -2 CORINTHIANS 6:14

Being "yoked" together is a farming example of two animals having a yoke, which is a wooden harness, that goes over the head of both animals and connects them together. The reason for this is because together, two animals can pull much more weight than if pulling by themselves. For instance, one horse can pull 1000 lbs., but 2 horses, together, can pull 10,000 lbs., so you can see the multiplication when two horses are equally yoked. Imagine now, you try to yoke a horse and an ox together. They are different heights, strengths, temperaments, etc. and even though they are two strong animals, by joining them together, you actually make them less effective, not more effective.

Marriage is a picture of two individuals who are supposed to be working together to multiply each other's strengths and effectiveness. If you have two single people playing marriage or have people of different faiths or no real faith, they will be pulling in different directions and minimizing each other's strengths. This then leads to arguments, strife, ongoing and increasing problems that will lead to many issues. Listen, even when two people have the same faith, marriage can be stressful, and you have to work through disagreements, but without this common faith and belief system, forget about it!

Light and dark are opposites and literally cannot co-exist. You can't have a bright light and darkness in the same place. With people of different faiths, or a person of faith and one with no faith, they often disagree about the most important things in life and at some point, they cannot agree nor walk together.

If both people are first in a committed relationship with Jesus, then He is shaping and molding them while He continues to knit their hearts together. The opposite is when both people try to change each other instead of focusing on changing themselves, which very predictably ends up with all kinds of bad dynamics leading to an eventual breakup. I needed God to change me and help me grow into everything He created me to be.

JESUS GIVES US FREEDOM

I wanted to be married. I wanted to be faithful. I wanted to do right things, but I was a slave to my sinful lifestyle. Yes, I can give reasons for what pushed me there, but I still had to deal with the reality of where I was. Many women tried to "set me free" but failed because that was a God-size job. Women fulfilled every sexual desire I had, but it wasn't enough. Many women reading this did all they could to please an unpleasable man. Let it go. You were trying to fill the Grand Canyon with a shovel and a pile of dirt! I drank the best alcohol and did the "best" drugs, but it didn't satisfy. Neither did money, my own business, the best car and on and on… none of it satisfied. I was a slave to my flesh and to sin, but Jesus set me free.

But now that you have been set free from sin and have become slaves of God, the benefit you reap leads to holiness, and the result is eternal life. -ROMANS 6:22

Let me break this down a little, in case you are not familiar with these Bible concepts; it's actually very simple. Being a slave to God just means that He is in charge of your life instead of sex, alcohol, money or anything else. He's the boss, nothing more, nothing less. Holiness means special and valuable, to be used for God's purposes, not to be used and abused by people who don't or can't appreciate you. Lastly, following God has benefits both now, on a daily basis, and also for eternity with God in heaven. God is always looking out for you.

LETTING GO OF REGRET

I have also wrestled with being mad at myself for the wasted years and the bad choices that I made. Yes, it is healthy to admit being wrong and realizing the bad decisions we make hurt us. Yes, we need to be responsible and own who we have been and what we did, but we also need to move on. When I realized that Jesus died on the cross and forgave all my sins, I knew that I had to come to a place where I forgave myself for every stupid thing I ever did! I realized that if I was ever to become the person God created me to be, I had to learn to let go of the past and move forward in a better direction.

FORGIVING YOURSELF

The reality is that any relationship is between two broken people. Chances are you may have to forgive yourself for one or more things.

Many women are mad at themselves because they got duped. They gave their heart to a man who did not count it as precious. Others have badgered men to change and may have either felt like they drove them away, or they actually did drive them away. Part of being healthy is recognizing mistakes, forgiving yourself and then correcting them. The fact that you are reading this book is evidence that you want to grow and are going in the right direction and moving towards better days.

You may be like I was, learning these things as an adult because you were never taught them as a child, teen or young adult. You may be like me; you heard some of these things in church but didn't understand or purposely chose not to follow them; forgive yourself. Even if you were like me, just flat out rebellious and have no one to blame but yourself for certain things, forgive yourself.

Even if you don't know how to forgive yourself, ask God to forgive you, because He already has. Forgiving yourself can also be a process, especially when you are still paying for bad decisions. This is why walking with God on a daily basis is key. Let Him strengthen you and heal you. Forgiveness will happen.

IT WAS NEVER YOUR JOB TO MAKE A MAN HAPPY

Remember, the Bible teaches about "the joy of the Lord". This means that the source of a person's joy is meant to be God. If someone is not receiving this joy from God, they will look to other inferior sources. This is why a man can't make a woman happy and a woman can't make a man happy. These come from God first. Then a spouse becomes a blessing, but a person's source remains God. So, first make sure you are receiving joy from your relationship with God, then realize your spouse is a blessing and an addition, but not your main or only source of happiness.

CHAPTER 23

HELPING YOUR MAN IN HIS BROKENNESS

I feel I am a good husband now, but that's because I faced my brokenness. But I also realize that each day my wife continues to help me become a better man. Years ago, I also realized that I had a lot to learn about treating a woman the way she deserved.

The reality is that many great women are totally committed to the men in their lives even when they have not been treated well. You may be dating or are married to a broken man. Let me be honest; we are all broken on some level. He may have many good attributes, but his brokenness and unfilled gaps will eventually sabotage any relationship if not rectified. No woman can fix everything, but if you are committed to your man and in actually helping him become whole and strong, you can be a vital part of the team. Please don't try to be the Savior; that job is already taken, but you if you are strategic, you can be a kingmaker.

YOU ARE WHERE YOU ARE

As you read this, you may be in a relationship or not. You may be dating or married. You may be living with a man and trying to make it work or trying to figure out a way to escape your current circumstances. You can't go back and change things, but you can absolutely move forward day by day into a better future! It all begins by going to God daily for your source of strength and guidance. If you don't do that, you will have to try to work things out in your own limited strength.

By nature, most women tend to be extremely faithful, nurturing and supportive. This can be either good or bad. Good because it can be powerful to help foster change or bad because it can accept poor behavior or even abuse. No matter where you are, my first recommendation is don't try to do things on your own. You not only need God, but you need people to support and encourage you on your way. This is where being part of a strong church can help you. Let me be real; some churches are much better at this than others. You may be reading this and have never really gone to church or you may have had a bad church experience. I encourage you to find a Bible believing and teaching church that will help you build a relationship with God and with people who will support and encourage you on your journey. You may also benefit greatly from an older woman who has traveled your road and would love to pray for and encourage you along the way.

GIVE SPACE OR HOLD ACCOUNTABLE?

So, as a woman, if you are in a relationship with a man, should you give him space to grow or hold him responsible for his words and actions? The answer is simple - yes. Before we get into the details, lets agree that abuse or mistreatment is never acceptable and should never be tolerated. But the reality is that there are a lot of low level disagreements and attitudes that couples have that we all wish would go away.

Giving space and holding people accountable are issues that are often more art than science. I can't tell you how much space to give and how strong to hold people accountable in every situation. Both are affected by many factors and this is where being led by God and using wisdom are needed. Bottom line is that we should all be held accountable for our actions and we all need time and space to grow. However, we must understand that being hypercritical or giving people forever to change will cause bigger problems in the future.

GIVING THE RIGHT AMOUNT OF SPACE

We have to be realistic. If a man hasn't been taught, shaped and trained to do things the right way, it will take him time to grow and change. There are changes that need to take place that will involve significant and often painful changes. No one likes change, and it is said that people don't change until the pain of staying the same is greater than the pain of change.

I needed to change over 30 years of ingrained thinking and behaviors which didn't surface overnight. I thank God now, but I hated the changes I was going through at the time. I had to deny my flesh for the first time in my life and it was so hard. I remember calling up my mentor and telling him that Christianity sucks! I was like a spoiled child who was being parented for the first time. I was a 6 foot 3, 220-pound baby!

The men of my church walked with me and were very wise on when to give me space and when to get in my face! They did and said things that I would not have received from a woman! Call it pride or ego, but most men are like this to some degree. This is why it is important for your man to follow Christ and be surrounded by strong men who won't be deterred when he struggles or pushes back. There is an emotional distance and hardness that men can receive from other men that is very helpful.

Please hear me on this, I am not saying women are not strong, but men speak a different language and can help men navigate their man thinking, emotions and responses. Trust me, if you can walk with a man through this type of change, you are VERY strong, even with getting this input from other men. If you are reading this, you are strong because you have not quit, and you want to grow and do things better!

HOLDING ACCOUNTABLE

One of the greatest things that has helped me to grow, change and constantly re-adjust and correct myself is accountability. At first, I learned this from the men in my church. One particular man took me under his wing. He served one of the pastors and I helped him serve them. Part of change takes humility and I had to learn humility before both God and men. I missed that lesson on the streets. This man also helped me understand why and how to follow God's Word. I had to learn as a follower of Christ, I was saying that I would be obedient to the Bible and the teachings of Jesus. This is one of the reasons why it is so important that a woman is with a man who is in relationship and follows Christ. All these things happened to me before I met my wife, otherwise, we wouldn't have lasted.

I learned to be accountable to God, His Word and other men of God. That's three huge sources and lessons on being responsible for myself. With this foundation, my wife can hold me accountable to God and His Word because I have committed to a personal relationship with Jesus. Before that, even if I did have good intentions towards women, they were temporary and were usually more of a means to get what I wanted.

Whether or not your man follows Christ, you still have the right to be treated well and to hold him accountable to being faithful to you, but most men, if they are not submitted to God and used to doing things how they want, will not be responsive to you in the long run. They either can't understand or may just be rebellious, and at some point, will be driven by their emotions and flesh. In fact, if they are not followers of Christ, they literally cannot understand the things of God.

WHAT DOES BORN AGAIN MEAN AND WHY IS IT IMPORTANT?

When I speak of a person having a relationship with Christ, it means that God gives them a new start in life. They were spiritually dead and empty, but God gives them the Holy Spirit and new life. That's why the Bible uses the word "born again" which describes a spiritual birth where sins are forgiven and God leads people by the power of the Holy Spirit. Without the Holy Spirit, a person literally cannot understand how God wants them to treat people.

The person without the Spirit does not accept the things that come from the Spirit of God but considers them foolishness, and cannot understand them because they are discerned only through the Spirit. -1 CORINTHIANS 2:14

For me, the idea of being faithful to a woman was foolishness, but after growing in my relationship with Jesus, I am truly committed to being faithful to my wife for the rest of my life.

You begin to see why God wants both men and women to be committed to Him first; He is shaping and molding them instead of the pattern of constant arguments and disappointments with each person trying to win. When I am focused on growing to be more like Jesus, I love my wife better.

A CHANGED MIND LEADS TO CHANGED BEHAVIORS

Changed behavior begins with a changed spirit. Then a changed spirit opens the door to a changed mind. If a man's thinking is incorrect and you want it to be correct, some major changes must take place. For the first 34 years of my life, I had never met a man who had been faithful to either their wife or girlfriend. My thinking was that you can be "committed" to a woman but still have other women on the side. As of the writing of this book, I have been 100% faithful to my wife of 7 years. Before this was possible, my thinking had to change.

ONLY GOD CAN TRULY CHANGE A HEART AND MIND

The reality is that we must continually go to God's Word to change our mind if we want to live differently and better. Many women tried to change my thinking, but only God was able to do that.

Women, without a doubt are often powerful influences in men's lives, but if a man is resistant to God, he will also be resistant to you. If a man's heart and mind are resistant or against God, at some point, it won't matter how great a woman you are; they may not receive your encouragement to be a better man.

Many women have felt insufficient or unworthy because a man or men have not responded to their positive efforts and their influences have not transformed men. Remember, God told you not to give your best to someone who does not have the ability to appreciate it. Notice that God's Word teaches us that we are transformed by the renewing of our minds through God's Word. If a man is not open to God's Word and God's power of transformation, change will be very limited and usually not final.

So, as you grow in faith and strength, encourage your man to do the same while giving him space to grow. Pray together, cry together, fall down and get up together.

THE IMPORTANCE OF PRAYER

When we can't fix things on our own, we need God's help.

"Prayer invites God's power into your situation. If you could fix it in your own strength it would already be fixed." -JACK REDMOND

So, prayer invites God into our situations to help us. We need his help to stay strong, to keep positive, to keep going.

ESCAPING THE BURNING BUILDING

God's Word teaches us to do everything we can to live peacefully with everyone:

If it is possible, as far as it depends on you,
live at peace with everyone. -ROMANS 12:18

But there are times when it doesn't matter what you do, some people don't want to live peacefully. Most women will put out 100 fires and keep rebuilding the house, but at some point, staying in a burning house is a losing game. If you keep putting out the fire and your man is sitting around lighting matches and pouring gas on your relationship, you must walk away. If a man refuses to change and you are forced to walk away, trust that God will bring the right man into your life. If you are dating or living with someone, but not married, this is simpler. Leaving an abusive, broken or simply dead-end relationship may actually be what's needed to make space for the right relationship.

If you are married, have children, etc. then you are all in, unless he is unfaithful. Many women will stay with a man even after he cheats. But keep in mind, God's will is never unfaithfulness and He doesn't expect you to endure that if he refuses to change. One thing I have seen over and over again is that God can heal any marriage if both people are willing to walk it out and change.

CHAPTER 24

HELPING YOUR SON WHEN DAD IS AWOL

Let's start with this fact – some of the greatest parents on earth are single mothers. We have so much respect for the single mothers who, most often, do an amazing job. Another truth is that raising a young man is challenging with two committed parents, so if you are struggling as a single mother, don't think that married women are raising young men without a lot of hard work and struggles too. But the reality is that a young man growing up without a strong father meeting his needs will have gaps. The biggest truth is that it's not your job to fill in every gap yourself, but you can be strategic in helping your son prepare for a successful life. Here are a couple of key things you can do that I have learned in my own life, working with youth, doing men's ministry locally and internationally, and now running a counseling center frequented by men who have huge gaps due to a lack of fathering.

BE THE BEST YOU

As a mother, you are an amazing and powerful gift from God to your son. Don't underestimate that – ever! Your job is to be you and do what God called you to do. Your son has a father whose responsibility it is to be a father; if he is not present, it is not your job to be your son's father. Maybe your son's father is not around, or you don't want him to be involved for whatever reason. We can't change yesterday, but we can make a better today and change what tomorrow will look like.

There are many things that your son needs that you can give. Especially when he is young, it is a mother's love and attention that is often the most important human need in a child's life. Give everything you have to be a great mother. Building this strong bond when a child is young will set the foundation for your relationship and parenting as your son grows older.

PROVIDE STRUCTURE AND DISCIPLINE

A child has a great need and benefits greatly from structure and discipline. Having rules and routines is a powerful tool in raising a child. When a child knows they are expected to act and behave a certain way, they develop strong standards that will last. When they are young, most children want to please their mother, and this is a time to make a lasting impact. As your son grows, yes, he will press his limits and try you, but if there is a strong bond of love and an established lifestyle of structure and discipline, this can greatly reduce rebellion and other problems.

DON'T TRY TO ALWAYS MUSCLE YOUR SON

One of the mistakes some mothers make is trying to muscle their sons too much. This works when a boy is small, but as he grows physically and intellectually, it becomes more ineffective. That's why I started with talking about love and structure. You want to lead your son, not drive him, to behaving properly. I have seen many single mothers over-utilize yelling and physical punishment, which gets desired results as a child, but when the boy hits 14-15 years old, you can't yell or spank a boy into submission on an ongoing basis. The goal is that they value your authority and are obedient by choice rather than you having to physically force proper behavior. I'm not saying you should never yell or physically discipline, but at some point, that becomes a losing strategy and will often encourage rebellion as he matures.

BE FINANCIALLY SMART

One of the hardest things for single mothers is living within your financial means. Many women make good money and understand budgeting and financial principles, but many don't. Staying out of debt and living within your means is very important. Many people are in need of learning about finances. There are many good resources out there to help you.

Don't spend money out of guilt. Sometimes people spend money they don't have because they feel bad. Our children must know the difference between necessity and luxury. A child needs sneakers, but they don't have to be $180 Air Jordan's. Your child needs your love and presence more than a pair of sneakers they will outgrow in three months.

On that note, please hold your son's father responsible to support his son financially. Some women feel bad about this, but you don't have to. Your father's son has a legal and moral responsibility to provide for his son. It is also not right that a woman has to work full time, raise their child and make many sacrifices while the man who fathered the child has no responsibility. The laws are on your side and he actually has no choice. Please don't let your son's father guilt trip or bully you so you don't hold him accountable. If you just let him ignore and neglect his responsibility to your son, it will hurt both you and your son. If this or anything else causes strife and arguments with your son's father, do all you can to talk, disagree and fight away from your son. Here is why.

YOUR SON SEES HIMSELF AS HIS FATHER'S SON

This can be a hard concept for a woman to understand and accept but let me explain. In some way, a boy is wired to value himself based on his father. So, in some ways, a son must believe in the goodness of his father. In many young boys' minds, if his father is not good, then neither is he. So, boys root for their father's success. They want their dad to be a winner.

So many boys hope that their father will do what's right and turn out good in the end because they are their father's son. So, if a mother tears down a boy's father, many boys will take it as an attack against them and the essence of who they are. They rationalize that "if my father is no good, then I am no good." There is something in a boy's mind that makes him want to be like his dad and more than anything else, they want their dad to be good. This can be very frustrating to a mom who surrenders her life for her child who doesn't always appreciate the sacrifice and then turns around when their absentee father shows up and the boy acts like they are great and can do no wrong. This is a picture of a starving boy getting vital nutrients and over reacting to the events. It is a broken boy having hope that his father is good which confirms that he too is good, and it is not a knock against you.

NO THIS ISN'T FAIR

No, it's not fair when a mother pays the price and at times more appreciation is given to a father who gave very little, but please try not to take it personally or let it hurt you. Yes, get upset, but do all you can to let it go. It is a product of dysfunctionality that will pass. As your son grows, he will see and appreciate all you have done.

BAD MOUTHING IS NOT THE ANSWER

Many women, especially those who have experienced bad things from their son's father, at some point, speak out against them. This is natural, and I am not saying it should never happen. Remember, we talked about accountability and responsibility of your son's father, but that is different from publicly criticizing and tearing them down. Some women have turned this into an art form and paid for it by driving their own sons away.

It was very confusing for me when my mother always said, "You are just like your father," and she said it all the time in both good and bad situations. *So, who is this man that I am so like? Is he as bad as you make him sound and am I that bad? Is he good and am I good? If I am good, why doesn't he want to be in my life?* I love my mom dearly, so it was very hard for me to hear these things from her and then to even be mad at her.

TRY TO CONNECT YOUR SON WITH OTHER MEN

This can take place on many levels. Sports was a great thing for me as my coaches praised me, corrected me, coached me and encouraged me to be my best. There were also uncles and others who were solid sources of encouragement for me as I grew. For me, the best place I have found to help me grow as a man and fill in the gaps has been my church. I wish I had connected with a church like this as a teen. I have seen many teens turn their lives around and connect with other men in our church.

Please remember that no man can replace a boy's father, but they can contribute to their lives. Try to find mentors to encourage your son's gifts. If it's sports, music, computers, or something else, you may be able to find someone to train them. Any type of discipline and responsibility will be beneficial.

ENCOURAGE YOUR SON TO DREAM

We live in America and while everything is not fair all the time, there are opportunities to do many things in our country and we should encourage our sons to do great things. In my life, I have owned a construction company, a mortgage company and now the Family Healing Center. I am a CEO and partner with million-dollar organizations on a regular basis. This is now my first book and I have travelled internationally on business and ministry. Don't ever get caught up on "the world's not fair." Whether or not the world is fair, I am going to excel and do great things and so should your son.

ENCOURAGE YOUR SON TO READ AND DO WELL IN SCHOOL

I was smart but not a good student. I got by on my brains, not my work ethic. I didn't get serious about education until I was in my thirties and went back to finish by undergraduate and then graduate degree. Not bad for a kid who got kicked out of junior high for bringing weed to school! So, be encouraged; if your son has made some mistakes, there is still hope.

If he is still young, read to him and encourage him to read. Yes, he can play sports and do many other things, but readers are leaders. If you can help him develop a passion for learning, you are setting a good direction for his life.

ENCOURAGE YOUR SON TO HAVE A RELATIONSHIP WITH JESUS

Something will be the driving force in your son's life. When it is God, his life will be better, period. My co-author was a youth pastor and quit working at the number one high school in the nation the week he received tenure to work at our church with teens. He did this because he saw the difference that Jesus made in teens lives, and it was worth walking away from a great career in a great school system because he understood the call of God on his life.

BE HAPPY!

One of the greatest things you can do to help your son is to be happy yourself! When your son sees you being happy, that will feed his soul. Being a mom is hard, period. Being a single mom can be even more challenging but enjoy the journey. Seek God with all your heart and trust that He will give you what your heart desires. God is your source for all things and the joy of the Lord is your strength! Life is a journey and there will be many bumps along the way. In the end, God has a plan and God has your back!

PRAYER FOR TRANSFORMATION

Father, I pray today for Your help. I pray that You fill in every gap that my earthly father did not fill in. I pray You teach me and send people to lead, mentor and coach me to be all You created me to be. I pray You also take all the good things that I have received from my father or family and use them to build up my family and I.

I pray that my family and I will overcome any injustices against my family and that You will heal any damage that has been done. I pray that any and all bad directions I or my family have chosen end, and that You lead me and my family in better directions.

Lord, You created me with a plan and purpose and I pray that You continually transform me to live out the purpose that You have already planned and created me to live – In Jesus Name I pray – Amen.

SALVATION PRAYER

Remember, it is not enough to just "believe in God." The real issue is whether or not you have realized that you are separated from God due to your own bad choices and actions. None of us are perfect and we all need a Savior. So, the question is "have you admitted your brokenness and wrong actions, want to live a better way and received the forgiveness of your sins through putting your faith in Jesus dying on the cross to pay for those sins?"

It's not about religion, it's about relationship! Is Jesus YOUR Lord and Savior? If not, but you understand what I just wrote about you can choose to follow Him right now. Can you remember a day when you asked Jesus to forgive you and commit to following Him? If that is what you desire, you can start by saying this prayer.

Jesus, I need and want You in my life. I know I have done many wrong things which have caused separation between You and I. Thank You for loving me so much that You died on the cross to pay for my sins. I ask for Your forgiveness right now. Come into my heart and cleanse it. Today, I choose to follow You. Help me to know You and give me the strength to walk with You. I pray this in Jesus name – Amen.

When you pray this prayer, God give you a new life, a new beginning with new direction. I pray you continue to walk with Him daily.

THERE IS ALWAYS HOPE

You may be reading this book, have a pretty good life and are just looking to make a few adjustments. Or you may be reading this, and your life looks like a train wreck with mangled metal and body parts everywhere you look. Either way, there is hope. You are breathing, there is a God who wants to help you and each day you get to decide the path you will take. If you are on the wrong path, have the courage to choose a better path. Many things, you can't fix or go back and change, but you can have a better future along with those that come after you. Keep moving forward, keep taking steps in the right direction, and watch what God can do with a broken life.

It's funny that even at my worst moments, somehow, I had hope. I can still remember my heart pounding during the cocaine seizure and wondering if my heart would explode and that would be the end. Somehow, I still had hope. I cried out to God and He answered. The second time I ended up in jail with a DUI, I felt like such a failure because I had sworn that I would never end up in jail again, but there I was. I couldn't have felt like a bigger loser, but I had hope.

One thing I have learned… what is not possible with men, is possible with God. When all of my natural strength was not enough, I learned to rely on God's supernatural strength. If you don't believe me, that's ok. I'm not mad at you. But I'm also not backing down because when everyone else failed me, God showed up!

DON'T LET WEIRD RELIGIOUS PEOPLE KEEP YOU FROM GOD

Let's be real, there are some weird religious folks out there! What my pastor has said many times is that people who are weird and religious were weird before they found God. Then he says, "Don't be weird!" My co-author, who is also a pastor at my church often says, "Don't let what people do, get in the way of what God wants to do." At the end of the day, you have to live your life, and you will either do this with God and with hope or without God and without hope.

IF YOU TRUST GOD, THERE IS ALWAYS HOPE

It took me awhile, but I learned that God does have a plan for people. When I say this, I am not talking about some type of vague religious belief that maybe things will be alright. I am talking about a personal Savior that gave up His life for me and you, so that we could live our purpose. Let's be real, I needed a BIG God to get me through my big problems and issues. Going to church wasn't enough, remember, I was a religious weekly church goer as a child, through college and as an adult. I needed a personal God to make a personal difference.

EMBRACE THE PROCESS

Let me end by saying that change is a process. It's not quick, and it's not easy, but it is worth it! If you are in a messed-up state, you went through a process to get there. You will probably need to fill in some holes, disentangle from some drama and go through a healing process. If you don't embrace and walk the process out, you will just keep doing the same things and getting the same results. Most people live very bold when they do wrong things; it's time to live bold when you do the right things. Remember, you can't erase the past, but you can definitely craft a brighter future.

ENDNOTES

1   https://www.brainyquote.com/quotes/jim_valvano_358465?src=t_father

2   www.google.com/dictionary/flounder

3   https://www.merriam-webster.com/dictionary/adolescent

4   https://www.ncbi.nlm.nih.gov/pmc/articles/PMC2794325/#__ref-listid312918title

5   http://www.dictionary.com/browse/adolescence

6   https://www.collinsdictionary.com/dictionary/english/arrested-development

7   Debra Dawson, "Family Structure…", *Journal of Marriage and Family*, No. 53. 1991.

8   http://lib.post.ca.gov/Publications/Building%20a%20Career%20Pipeline%20Documents/Safe_Harbor.pdf

9   US D.H.H.S. news release, March 26, 1999

10   U.S. Department of Health and Human Services press release, Friday, March 26, 1999

11   Carol W. Metzler, et al. "The Social Context for Risky Sexual Behavior Among Adolescents," Journal of Behavioral Medicine 17 (1994).

12   http://www.loveyoufather.com/fathersday-poems/whatmakes-a-dad.html

13   http://www.lifenews.com/2010/09/28/nat-6733/

14   http://whensteeltalks.ning.com/forum/topics/a-ship-without-a-captain-be-it-good-or-bad-cannot-sail-by-leon-fo?id=2534462:Topic:579554&page=2

15   https://www.goodreads.com/quotes/tag/self-identity

16   Redmond, Jack. *Wounded Heart*. Xulon Press, 2009.

17   https://www.brainyquote.com/quotes/friedrich_nietzsche_101616

18   White Men Can't Jump, 1992

19   https://mentalhealthdaily.com/2015/02/18/at-what-age-is-the-brain-fully-developed/

20   http://www.wiseoldsayings.com/time-heals-quotes/

21   James, John/Friedman, Russell. *The Grief Recovery Handbook: 20th Anniversary Addition*. Harper Collins, 2009.

22   https://www.psychologytoday.com/us/blog/here-there-and-everywhere/201208/25-quotes-anger

ABOUT THE AUTHORS

Malik Carey, M.S. is the CEO and founder of the Family Healing Center (www.FamilyHealingCenterNJ.com), author, keynote speaker, entrepreneur, consultant and life coach. As the founder and CEO of the Family Healing Center, he has personally built and led a team of psychiatrists, licensed social workers, counselors and life coaches to help individuals and families live better lives. He has a Master's degree in Organizational Leadership from Nyack College and a B.A. in Sports Management from Seton Hall University.

His experience has ranged from working with troubled inner-city youth, to personally coaching high-level organizational leaders of major corporations. He is also the former National Vice President and Chief Operating Officer of a national men's ministry named K.I.N.G. He has travelled throughout the United States and overseas for leadership training and men's ministry. He lives in northern New Jersey with his wife Deidra Carey.

Malik can be reached at: **www.MalikCareyCEO.com** for speaking and consulting requests.

- Keynote Speaker
- Organizational Consultant
- Life Coaching for personal or business
- Conference Speaker

Jack Redmond, M.Div., M.Ed. is an author, speaker, certified life coach and church building consultant. He is also the Church Mobilization Pastor at Christ Church, a multi-site 9000-member church located in New Jersey. He is a sought-after speaker for conferences, leadership development, evangelism and church growth training. He has authored or co-authored eight books. His leadership trainings have been hosted throughout the United States and overseas in Nicaragua and India. He and his wife Antoinette, live in New Jersey with their four children.

Jack can be reached at: **www.JackRedmond.org** for speaking and consulting requests.

- Keynote Speaker
- Organizational Consultant
- Life Coaching for personal or business
- Conference Speaker
- Church leadership and structure development

OTHER BOOKS BY JACK REDMOND

The 21 Laws of Evangelism: Biblical Principles Guaranteed to Turn the World Upside Down (Jack Redmond Ministries, 2017)

Transformed: 7 Pillars of a Legacy Minded Man (Racine, Wisconsin, BroadStreet Publishing, 2016)

Let Your Voice Be Heard: Transforming from Church Goer to Active Soul Winner (New York: Morgan James Publishing, 2016)

God Belongs in My City in partnership with Urban Kingdom Youth Ministries and www.GodBelongsInMyCity.com 2011

Infusion: Receive. Grow. Give it Away... (Alachua, FL: Bridge Logos, 2010)

Wounded Heart: Keys to Overcoming Life's Pain and Disappointment (Maitland, FL: Xulon Press, 2009)

People Matter to God: Experiencing Personal Transformation and Sharing it with Others (Maitland, FL: Xulon Press, 2008)

Me and my Dad celebrating my marriage. 6/25/11.

My Masters Degree Graduation. Three generations. 11/15/14.

*Me and my Dad in Hawaii the day we played all day
like two kids in the water. 5/24/15.*

Made in USA - Kendallville, IN
1225221_9781727760958
01.14.2021 1437